my
little
red
book

my

little

red

book

Edited by
RACHEL KAUDER NALEBUFF

TWELVE

NEW YORK   BOSTON

Twelve
Hachette Book Group
237 Park Avenue
New York, NY 10017

Visit our Web site at www.HachetteBookGroup.com.

Twelve is an imprint of Grand Central Publishing.
The Twelve name and logo are trademarks of Hachette Book Group, Inc.

Printed in the United States of America

First Edition: February 2009

10 9 8 7 6 5 4 3 2 1

Library of Congress Cataloging-in-Publication Data

Nalebuff, Rachel Kauder.
  My little red book / Rachel Kauder Nalebuff. — 1st ed.
      p. cm.
  Includes bibliographical references and index.
  ISBN 978-0-446-54636-2 (alk. paper)
  1. Adolescence. 2. Adolescent psychology. 3. Menstruation. I. Title.
  HQ796.N28 2009
  305.235'2—dc22
                                2008040621

Book design and text composition by L&G McRee

To mothers, especially mine

Contents

Introduction   1

Stories

Oh, Brother, 1993   13
—Louise Story, Cos Cob, CT

Good-bye, Green Thumb, 1942   14
—Thelma Kandel, New York, NY

Burning Secret, 1966   15
—Suzan Shutan, East Haven, CT

Fear of Fourteen, 1991   16
—Erica Jong, New York, NY

The Lie, 1948   20
—Shalom Victor, Santa Cruz, CA

Germany, 1942   21
—Nina Bassman, Queens, NY

The Artist, 1968   23
—Nina Bentley, Westport, CT

Bloody Bat Mitzvah, 2002   24
—Sarah Rosen, New Haven, CT

Going to X-tremes, 1982   25
—Michele Jaffe, Los Angeles, CA

blood relative, 1976   27
—Sondra Freundlich-Hall, San Francisco, CA

Too Wet, 1994   28
—Rafia

Guatemala: Advice from a Cheesemaker, 1953   30
—Flori, Chicago, IL

Mehn-su, 1992   31
—Amy H. Lee, Berkeley, CA

Can I Just Skip This Period? 1971   32
—Patty Marx, New York, NY

Silence, 1930s   34
—Elizabeth Siciliano, Cleveland, OH

A Jealous Vajayjay, 1981   34
—Nancy L. Caruso, Cardiff, CA

Into the Woods, 1964   38
—Sharon Gerhard, Novato, CA

Loss and Gain of Responsibility, 1969   40
—Zannette Lewis, Richmond, VA

The Ming Period, 1999   43
—Aliza Shvarts, Los Angeles, CA

Andy Roddick's Serve, 2003   45
—Jen Bashian, Los Angeles, CA

An Invisible Period, 1981   46
—S., New York, NY

Oh, the "Joy" of Menses! 1987   46
   —Megan McCafferty, Princeton, NJ

The Blusher, 2002   49
   —Elli Foster, Lancaster, PA

Hot Dog on a String, 1993   51
   —Ellen Devine, Wallingford, CT

Chairman Mao's Period, 1967   56
   —Xiao Ling Ma, Nanjing, China

LOL {.}, 2005   57
   —Zoe Kauder Nalebuff, New Haven, CT

Blood on the Tracks, 1972   58
   —Patricia E. Boyd, Pittsburgh, PA

Ink Blots and Milk Spots, 1987   59
   —Krista Madsen, Brooklyn, NY

Glamorous, but Not for Long, 1981   64
   —Jennifer Baumgardner, New York, NY

I Know You Are Not There, God. It's Me, Kate, 1990   66
   —Kate Zieman, Toronto, Canada

The Curse, 1939   69
   —Lola Gerhard, San Francisco, CA

The Simple Vase: Part I, 1997   71
   —Laura Wexler, New Haven, CT

The Simple Vase: Part II, 1997   74
   —Rebecca Wexler, New York, NY

Let Down, 2007   75
   —Tatum Travers, Chicago, IL

Desperately Delayed, 1970   76
    —Judy Nicholson Asselin, Westtown, PA

Proper Disposal, 1993   79
    —Catherine Conant, Middletown, CT

Mattress Pad, 1990   80
    —Yulia, New York

No Gushing for Me, Please, 1979   82
    —Monica Wesolowska, Berkeley, CA

The Slap, 1972   83
    —Ilene Lainer, New York, NY

Rescued by a Refugee, 1941   85
    —Pearl Stein Selinsky, Sacramento, CA

The Wrath of the Gods, 1970   86
    —Jill Bialosky, Cleveland, OH

Locked in a Room with Dosai, 1962   88
    —Shobha Sharma, Chennai, India

Simple as Salt, 1967 and 2008   92
    —Jacquelyn Mitchard, Madison, WI

Señorita, 1980   94
    —Kica Matos, New Haven, CT

Can I Sit on His Lap? 1916   96
    —Henrietta Wittenberg, New York, NY

Barbies and Biology, 1996   97
    —Aysegul Altintas, Istanbul, Turkey

An excerpt from "Letters"   99
    —Maxine Kumin, New Hampshire

My Support System Was a Box, 1977   101
   —Bonnie Garmisa, Guilford, CT

Jaws, 2004   102
   —Lily Gottchalk, Wallingford, CT

Dying in the Land of Dionysus, 1972   104
   —Mary Hu, New Haven, CT

Step Toward Womanhood, but with Stepmom, 1983   106
   —Lisa Selin Davis, Brooklyn, NY

Yodelay Uh-Oh, 1982   108
   —Cecily von Ziegesar, Brooklyn, NY

The White Dress, 1971   111
   —Kathi Kovacic, Cleveland, OH

Up at the Chalkboard, 1979   112
   —Emilia Arthur, Accra, Ghana

If Men Could Menstruate   114
   —Gloria Steinem, New York, NY

A Puddle, 1991   118
   —Laura Madeline Wiseman, Arizona

Out of the Closet, 1968   119
   —Joyce Maynard, Mill Valley, CA

Staining the Citroën, 1970   125
   —Catherine Johnson-Roehr, Bloomington, IN

Cranberry Sauce, 1993   127
   —Barclay Rachael Gang, Miami, FL

Tsihabuhkai, 1962   129
   —Juanita Pahdopony, Lawton, OK

The Dream, 1994   132
—Annie Sherman, Chico, CA

Operation Menstruation! 1998   133
—Jennifer Asanin Dean, Hamilton, Canada

Crushed Leaves in Kenya, 2006   135
—Thatcher Mweu, Nairobi, Kenya

Where's My Belt? 1979   136
—Meg Cabot, Bloomington, IN

My Second First Period, 1977   139
—Bernadette Murphy, Los Angeles, CA

Memory: Day 1, 1973   144
—M. Eliza Hamilton Abegunde, Evanston, IL

A Coup at the Napkin Dispenser, 1960   145
—Linda Lindroth, New Haven, CT

Downward Dog, 2004   147
—Marian Firke, Chicago, IL

The Harness, 1961   149
—Deo Robbins, Santa Cruz, CA

The Von Trapps and Me, 1980   149
—Debby Dodds, Los Angeles, CA

Dress Appropriately, 1974   153
—Bita Moghaddam, Pittsburgh, PA

The Earache, 1975   155
—Dr. Miriam Nelson, Medford, MA

Progressive Parenting, 1993   156
—Nancy Gruver and Joe Kelly, Duluth, MN

Showdown at the HoJo, 1968   159
—Linda Greenberg, Chicago, IL

No Longer in Little League, 1993   161
—Moira Kathleen Ray, Portland, OR

Euro Disney, 1992   161
—Jessy Schuster, Miami, FL

On Horseback, 1960s   163
—Margaret Whitton, Martha's Vineyard, MA

Not Getting It, 1980   165
—Rachel Vail, New York, NY

The Mermaid, 1974   168
—Sara Hickman, Austin, TX

When you phoned home from California
to tell me it had started   170
—Penelope Scambly Schott, Portland, OR

Peanut Butter and Chocolate Milk, 1959   171
—Kathrine Switzer, New Zealand and New York, NY

Tamora Pierce Saves the Day, 2006   172
—Madeleine, New York, NY

Slippery in the Stairwell, 1965   173
—Tamora Pierce, New York

Down Under, 1983   175
—Jenni Deslandes, Sydney, Australia

Time for Prayer, 2006   177
—Fatema Maswood, Cromwell, CT

The Right Place at the Right Time, 1952   178
—Leigh Bienen, Evanston, IL

Blood Month, 1979   179
   —Sandra Guy, Paris, France

Late Bloomer, 1998   187
   —Emily Hagenmaier, Los Angeles, CA

History Sometimes Repeats Itself, 1970   188
   —Marianne Bernstein, Philadelphia, PA

Twelve-Step Program, 1946   189
   —Marcia Nalebuff, Newton, MA

Flow, 1983   191
   —Tonya Hurley, New York, NY

You Always Remember Your First   194
   —Carla Cohen, Washington, DC

Euphemisms and Code Words   195

Learn More   197

Do More   199

Acknowledgments   203

Permissions   207

Indexes

   Subject   209

   Author   217

Reading Group Guide   221

About the Editor   225

Introduction

Every woman remembers her first period—where and when it happened, who, if anyone, she told, even what she was wearing. And yet, despite vivid memories of this momentous occasion, almost no one talks about it. Even fewer people write about it.

Why? Because first periods are an awkward subject. *My Little Red Book* is here to change that. This book is an effort to help us embrace the awkwardness and thereby end it. Think about it this way: if Napoleon Dynamite can be cool, so can periods.

As a first step, we can record our own stories and share them. The first-period stories in *My Little Red Book* are drawn from women across different generations and diverse backgrounds. The authors hail from New York to Nanjing, and the stories range from a tween's IM conversation to a grandmother's reminiscence about the days before tampons. There are stories about slaps, sharks, little brothers, plumbing accidents, yoga, and getting out of math exams.

You may be wondering how I, a seemingly normal eighteen-year-old, ended up collecting stories about menstruation. I like to think that *My Little Red Book* is the result of the best mistake that ever happened to me. It all started with my first period.

I was twelve and visiting my widowed and rather stiff grandfather in Boynton Beach, Florida. I was waterskiing when I first noticed a brown stain spreading steadily across the territory of my yellow bathing suit. My interpretations of the evolving Rorschach blot on my butt led me to the logical conclusion that I must have sat on something, like mud or maybe beets. As I was in the middle of the lake, I had to ski all the way back to shore before I could go to the bathroom to investigate further. Once in the privacy of the lakeside stall, I started to break down. This wasn't just some *schmutz* on my bathing suit. This was my period. *Aaaah!!!!*

No need to panic, I told myself; there was a cardboard stick that would solve all my problems. But twenty-five cents later, I was even more confused. Where did it go, how would I take it out, and most important, how would I clean up the mess?

My mother would certainly have the answers. I dialed her number. Ten times. No answer. Next I tried calling my grandmother. She valiantly attempted to coach me through the intricacies of tampon insertion. But it had been years since her last period, and her directions of "maybe a little bit to the left?" confirmed that this was the blind leading the blind. Frustrated and defeated, I stuffed my bathing suit with paper towels and waddled back to the boat, determined to finish my afternoon of waterskiing without telling anyone that I had gotten my you-know-what. Let's just say that waterskiing while trying to cover your butt could be classified as a new type of dance.

After all the paper towels had disintegrated and we were headed home, my grandfather made an unexplained detour. We ended up at the local pharmacy, where he reluctantly acknowledged what was going on by sputtering in his native French that I should go ask someone for assistance. His embarrassment was contagious, and I was too ashamed to approach anyone for help.

Perhaps because I didn't ask, or perhaps because the Boynton Beach community experiences more incontinence than menstruation, the closest thing I could find to a pad was its distant relative, Depends. Here I was, finally all grown up, and back to wearing a diaper—not exactly the way I had imagined greeting womanhood.

When I finally did reach my mother, we had a good laugh and cry together. To my horror, she decided to share my tear-filled account with . . . everyone. At the next family gathering, my first-period trauma was the topic of dinner discussion. I had been betrayed.

But then something amazing happened. The women in my family starting sharing their stories with each other and with me. I learned that my grandmother discovered her first period by noticing a trail of red drops on the stairs. (See "Twelve-Step Program," page 189) I knew that my great-aunt Nina had fled Poland to escape being deported to a concentration camp. But I never knew that she got her first period on that trip, and that it saved her from being strip-searched by Nazis at the German border. (See "Germany, 1942," page 21) The most amazing part of her story was that before she shared it with me, she had never told anyone—not her children, not her friends, no one.

With a sense of urgency, I realized that there was a whole generation whose stories would never be told unless someone did something. And so, for the sake of posterity, I decided to commit social suicide and started asking about first periods. Although my questions made some women cringe, the replies made it all worthwhile. With each new story, I felt that I had stumbled upon buried treasure that deserved to be shared. Thus began *My Little Red Book*.

Here I have assembled the very best stories I heard. Imagine how Magellan saw the earth, Galileo looked at the stars, or Sophie Kinsella shops for high heels, and you will understand how I have come to feel about first-period stories—an infinite collection just waiting to be discovered. This book is an effort to bring periods into the arena of acceptable discourse so that all of us can gather and share these experiences without a smidgen of self-consciousness.

In a world where we've embraced *The Vagina Monologues*, where *Juno* wins an Oscar and, hell, where we've even seen Janet Jackson's right nipple, girls have no reason to feel ashamed of their bodies. As Katherine Mansfield puts it in *Bliss and Other Stories*, "Why be given a body if you have to keep it shut up in a case like a rare, rare fiddle?" It is time for the menstruation monologues.

That could have been the book's title. Instead, I wanted to evoke Mao's *Little Red Book,* the manifesto distributed to all Chinese citizens during the Cultural Revolution. *My Little Red Book* shares the revolutionary spirit of its Chinese namesake—minus the communist propaganda. It is a call to literary arms to reclaim our rightful history. It also makes for a nice bedside companion.

For those of you who have just gotten or are about to get your first period, this book will help you know what to expect and remind you that you are not alone. Hopefully, it will open your eyes to the women around you and let you see that even your bingo-playing grandma was once in your same situation. Of course, you don't have to be a girl to enjoy *My Little Red Book*. These stories speak to universal experiences: dealing with parents, connecting with one's cultural identity, feeling inadequate around siblings, being put on the spot, and grappling with growing up.

As I read these stories, I find myself coming back to the same questions: Why is there so little celebration of the event? What does a woman's first-period experience reveal about her character? And is there anyone who *hasn't* read Judy Blume's *Are You There God? It's Me, Margaret?*

Blume's tweenage saga seems to be the bible for girls going through puberty. That's understandable; for many contributors, Blume's book was their main source of information regarding first periods. For Meg Cabot (see page 136), this meant believing that girls still wore belted pads, just like Margaret did. This leads me to conclude that it's time we updated and expanded our first-period canon. As Mao famously said, "Let a hundred flowers bloom."

These stories teach us more than the facts of life. As Michele Jaffe observes in "Going to X-tremes" (page 25), how a girl handles her first period says a lot about who she is and who she will become. Artist Nina Bentley's instinct to draw a flower out of her stain was a sign of her future career (page 23). Bita Moghaddam's frustration that only girls get periods foreshadowed her feminism (page 153).

Most of all, the stories leave me wondering, *Where's the period party at?* Too often, menarche marks a somber occasion. In her story "Loss and Gain of Responsibility" (page 40), Zannette Lewis writes that menarche historically marked the age at which a slave could be sold off as a woman. In "The Harness" (page 149), Deo Robbins describes feeling humiliated when she first stepped into her mother's sanitary napkin. Several stories recount the pain of being slapped upon sharing the news.

Unfortunately, the taboo of menstruation is embedded in our religions, culture, and history. The Quran (2:222) declares that menstruating women "are a hurt and a pollution" and orders men to "keep away from women in their courses, and do not approach them until they are clean." Jewish women are forbidden to have sex. French housewives can't make mayonnaise and, as Shobha Sharma describes in her story "Locked in a Room with Dosai" (page 88), Indian women are exiled from their own homes. Even the great philosophers touched on the subject. In ancient Rome, Pliny the Elder wrote that menstrual blood "turns new wine sour, crops touched by it become barren, grafts die, seeds in gardens are dried up, the fruit of trees fall off, the edge of steel and the gleam of ivory are dulled."[1]

Today, Pliny seems ridiculous, but discrimination and ignorance remain. The problems go well beyond being told to sit out during gym. In Pakistan, 87 percent of girls haven't heard about menstruation prior to their first period.[2] In Africa, a lack of sanitary supplies often forces girls to stay home from school during their periods, thereby depriving them of almost a quarter of their rightful education.[3] And then there are the various African tribes that mark a girl's first period as the date for genital mutilation.

That is not to say that we haven't made headway or that there aren't any cultures that commemorate the occasion. Take the Navajo, for example. *Kinaalda*, the celebration of a woman's first period, is one of their most important ceremonies. The four-day-long ritual is filled with joyous dance and song. If men had periods, you can bet that they would celebrate. This is the point of Gloria Steinem's classic essay "If Men Could Menstruate" (updated for us on page 114), in which she imagines how men would glorify their periods.

1. Pliny, *Natural History*, trans. H. Rackham (Cambridge, MA: Harvard University Press, 1961), book 7, p. 549.

2. "Adolescence in Pakistan: Sex, Marriage and Reproductive Health," *Marie Stopes Society Journal* (2006).

3. Royalties from *My Little Red Book* are being donated to help address this problem; to learn more, see page 199.

Of course, we don't have to brag or throw stag parties. Celebrating might just mean telling your mom.

Even if you've missed the first opportunity to celebrate, each month provides a new chance. Isn't it mysterious that women living together get their periods in sync? Though our connection to the moon may not be scientific, it is empowering nonetheless. This monthly mutual "suffering" should bond and inspire us. No one puts it better than Erica Jong when she explains in *What Do Women Want?* that "the very source of my inspiration lies in my never forgetting how much I have in common with other women, how many ways in which we all are similarly shackled." Indeed, Krista Madsen cites "the beautiful untidiness of being a woman" as a constant theme in her work, reappearing and reinventing itself each time she writes. Many contributors have told me that writing their first-period story was deeply introspective, calling forth buried childhood memories, and a sense of identity and connection with all women. Periods are powerful stuff.

My hope is that this book will help you start a dialogue with the women around you. I see the importance of this communication in my own life; talking about first periods has transformed my lunch-table conversations from gossip to discussions of women's rights. For many contributors, writing their own stories prompted them to ask their mothers for their stories or talk more openly with their daughters. Two sets of mothers and daughters were even inspired to send in stories together (see "The Simple Vase:

Parts I and II," "Into the Woods," and "The Curse"). By airing our own stories, we open channels of communication between women—mothers and daughters, sisters and aunts—and turn a taboo into a cause for celebration. The dialogue has already begun.

Continuing it is up to you.

RACHEL KAUDER NALEBUFF
New Haven, Connecticut

Stories

Oh, Brother, 1993

The chronology: I learn, I cry, I wish, I get, I divulge.

Third grade: Mom tells me about periods as we drive past the Mobil station and frozen yogurt store. I glare at the red stoplight, feeling angry. I didn't want to know about this. I don't want a period to happen to me. Pimples would not happen, breasts would not, and definitely not periods.

Fourth grade: Mom shoves giant pads into my suitcase as I head to summer camp. Just in case. Again, she tells me what I would do if "it" comes, and again, I hate hearing about it. Why does she keep talking about this? I do not want to share the big female secret, not yet, not ever.

Sometimes, she sends my dad out to buy tampons. "Soon he'll be buying them for two," she says. It takes me a few moments to realize that the other woman would be me.

Fifth grade: My seventh-grade friend is over, and I'm eager to impress her. Periods, I know, are for teenagers. I dump an entire bottle of neon pink perfume on my underwear and run out to find her. But she laughs at the stain, even as I ask: "Is it my period?" She tells me to talk to my mom about it. Too embarrassed of my forged blood, I throw the undies away.

Seventh grade: My period comes for real, and it is not neon pink. Thanks to Mom, there are four-year-old gigantic pads still under my sink, where I put them after summer camp. I waddle around for a day, then ask my mom for tampons. I am now that other woman.

Eighth grade: My nine-year-old brother comes into my room and tells me that my mom sent him to learn about periods.

"Really?" I ask. "Why didn't she tell you about it herself?"

"I don't know, Louise, she just told me to ask you."

Reluctantly, I launch into an explanation and even show him what tampons and pads look like. I feel emotional just telling it. I can't help thinking I've done a good job when I finish.

Later on, I ask my mom why she sent my brother to me for an explanation.

"I didn't. Why would I?" she asks.

I realize I've been duped.

"You didn't tell him anything, did you, Louise?"

—Louise Story, Cos Cob, CT

Louise Story is a staff writer for the New York Times, *where she covers Wall Street. She likes to refer to her period as "my communist friend."*

Good-bye, Green Thumb, 1942

When I got my period, my father told me I should not water the plants, otherwise they would die.

—Thelma Kandel, New York, NY

Thelma is a mixed-media artist and author of What Women Earn *and* What to Name the Cat.

Editor's Note: Taboos preventing menstruating women from planting or gardening have existed in various cultures since biblical times. According to *The Curse: A Cultural History of Menstruation*, some scientists in the 1920s went so far as to claim that menstruating women excreted plant-killing "menotoxins." All attempts to replicate their research failed.

Burning Secret, 1966

I was eleven years old and the first of all my friends to get a period. Since most girls didn't seem to get a period until they were twelve, thirteen, or fourteen years old, my parents and my friends' parents had not bothered to bring up the subject for discussion. I had no idea what a period was. When older girls said the word, I just thought they were talking about sentence structure. One summer afternoon when I was home alone, I felt sticky between my legs, as if I had peed in my pants. I went into the bathroom, pulled down my underwear, and was stunned to discover them drenched with blood. I knew then that I was dying.

I was okay about dying, but thought my parents and friends might be upset, so I kept my dying a secret. I told no one. Every day for eleven days, close to sunset, I took off the blood-drenched underwear and shorts or pants through which the blood had seeped, went outside to our trash cans hidden behind a fence bordering some woods, and set fire to the bloody objects, watching them burn until they turned to ash.

On the twelfth day, I was caught. My mom discovered me, my fire, and the last vestige of my last pair of underwear. She questioned why I would burn my underwear. Naturally, I could not tell her that I was dying, so I refused to speak. She grew angry, marched me into her bedroom, and demanded that I explain to my father why I was burning my underwear. My silence provoked fury, and together my parents began taking away privileges until I was left with not even the possibility of going outside. So I told them. I was bleeding . . . I was dying . . . and I was sparing them my pain.

—Suzan Shutan, East Haven, CT

Suzan is a visual artist who exhibits nationally and regionally. She likes to refer to her period as "the untimely moment."

Fear of Fourteen, 1991

Some people believe that women are more connected to nature than men are. We seem to have less squeamishness about blood and pee and poop—at least some of us. And that's probably good because we will go through many metamorphoses in our lives, and blood will be part of them. We can't afford to be afraid of blood. We have to treat it as a marker of maturity.

This stuff of life is connected with our ability to make

babies, and it always amazes me to see how many times women's bodies transform themselves. It's utterly miraculous that we go from round to flat to round to flat again. And maybe all this makes us more flexible and less fearful. We understand that life *is* metamorphosis. This is a very good thing to know. We are always changing. All wisdom is in understanding that.

Childhood is hardly without its terrors—both solitary and social. But it all comes to a horrible head in middle school. The kids get meaner, and teen angst makes us more vulnerable. It's puberty that does it, or the fear of puberty. Girls with breastlets lord it over girls with flat chestlets. If you were not born knowing about tampons and menstruation, you are considered a *retard*.

Once, in summer camp, I conspired with a group of girls to press ripe cherries into the clean white crotch of another girl's underwear. She put on the panties and freaked, thinking she had her first period. What a rotten thing to do! Did I speak up for her? No. I was as rotten as the rest. I probably *thought up* the devilish prank and now am trying to suppress that memory. We can all be equally rotten at that stage of life.

My daughter Molly was no exception. We were traveling in Italy the summer she was thirteen going on fourteen. I wanted to take her to see Florence, and particularly the lovely villa where I had studied Italian when I was a teenager. The place was called the Torre di Bellosguardo and it sat on a verdant hill above Florence, looking down on the

Duomo. Paths with vines led down to the outskirts of the city. Everything was a sun-dappled green and white.

We drove the autostrada from Venice, arrived in the late afternoon, and were lucky to get the last available room in the hotel the villa had become. But the room had no air-conditioning, and Molly was pissed. We went down to the pool to take a dip. Florence was sweltering. Our T-shirts stuck to our backs.

"What a horrible pool!" Molly said. "And we have a hideous, hot room. I can't imagine why you wanted to come to this godforsaken place!"

Here I had wanted to share precious memories with Molly, and she would have none of it. I was devastated.

She complained and complained until I did what I had never done before or since—I emptied a cold bottle of San Pellegrino on her head. She fled to the outdoor ladies' room in a fit of pique, and in a little while I could hear her summoning me to the bathroom.

"Mommy, look!" she said, showing me a tissue with bright red blood on it. Then she threw her arms around me, saying, "Mommy, I love you soooo much!"

We stayed up all night that night, talking about a million things we had never really discussed before: my divorce from her father, her infancy, and even my first period.

"We were on the *Île-de-France*, returning to New York from a holiday in France," I told Molly, "and suddenly, it was *there*. My mother used to call it 'getting unwell'—which I thought was an antique expression. I used so many pads and tissues that I kept stuffing up the toilet. The purser used to come in and scold me horribly in French. I was so embarrassed. He had to unblock my toilet again and again. I felt that the whole ship resounded with my shame.

"'Now you'll be able to have babies,' my mother had said—which didn't make me feel any better. And then she gave me a big slap on the behind.

"'What's that for?' I asked.

"'It's supposed to be good luck,' she said.

"'Why?' I asked."

"Yeah, why?" Molly echoed.

"My mother believed in every *bubbameiseh* from every culture. She couldn't have enough superstitions—especially unpleasant ones to ward off the evil eye."

"That's Grandma," Molly said.

"And it's a damned good thing you never whacked me on the butt!" she added.

"If I didn't know what it meant, why should I do it?"

"Right," said my daughter. "Superstition has to stop *somewhere*."

—Erica Jong, New York, NY

Erica Jong is a critically acclaimed writer and poet. She is a pioneer in progressive feminist literature and the author of twenty books, including the best-selling novel Fear of Flying. *In her 2006 work,* Seducing the Demon: Writing for My Life, *Jong reflects upon her early life and provides advice for writers. Her most recent work is* Love Comes First, *a volume of poetry published in January 2009.*

The Lie, 1948

Every day I examined my underwear, looking for the dark maroon blemish that other girls my age talked about. I was thirteen and wanted to be just like everyone else; to be included in the circle of girls who had become women. Although some balked about the mess and the stomachache, this was something I coveted, something that felt unreachable to me.

Humiliated and thinking myself outside of God's natural laws, I lied.

My mother asked, "When?"

"At school," I said, shrugging my shoulders, as if to convey that it was no big deal. My mother questioned me no further, as I suspect she was prudish, although I did see a slight smile cross her face. We were not close and lacked the easy friendship that some girls enjoyed with their mothers.

I overheard school chums say, "Oh, God, I almost died, it got all over the back of my skirt." I got into the conversation then.

"Oh, yes," I said, shaking my head, "that happened to me, too. Wasn't it awful?" I felt guilty about my lie, and also terribly worried that I would never become one of them.

By the time I was going on fifteen, having gotten no results from quiet prayer in my bedroom, I ascended the stairs to the roof of our four-story tenement building. I looked at the other rooftops, the wired cage at the top of the elementary school I once attended, and stretched out my arms toward the firmament and prayed.

"Dear God, please give me my period (which I thought was rightfully mine), please! I just want to be part of the crowd!" I tacked on an additional prayer. "Could you also give me breasts while you're at it?"

Two days later, I awoke to a sticky feeling in my pajama bottoms. When I pulled them down, I already knew what was there. I felt inexpressible joy. I changed my pants and ran into the bathroom to locate my mother's stash of Modess pads. I tucked one into my panties and found I could hardly walk. I felt that I was sitting astride a couch cushion.

Unfortunately for me this true time, there was no one to tell.

—Shalom Victor, Santa Cruz, CA

Originally from the Bronx, Shalom Victor is currently working on Following the Leader, *a book about what it was like to be part of a cult group in the 1970s. She is a grandmother of five.*

Germany, 1942

I was thirteen. It was 1942. We were fleeing Poland and the deportation of the Jews.

The atrocities committed by the Germans were getting worse. Ghettos were being formed. My uncles in Belgium and France went through enormous troubles to obtain visas and passage for us to get out. To reach Belgium, we had to pass through Germany. My story takes place on the train arriving from Poland at the German border crossing. The train stopped, and we were told to get completely undressed for the customs guards to search us.

The guards were mostly searching for hidden jewelry, and they looked in the most private places. It was horrible. I had hidden my yellow Star of David in my shoe, but it was discovered. In my fright, I completely lost it and peed in my pants. But when I looked down, what I saw was actually a stream of red. I raced into the compartment, and my mother saw what was happening. She rushed to the toilets at the end of the train and grabbed lots of rolls of toilet paper, one of which she shoved into my underwear. She was somehow able to do this so discreetly that my two sisters and brother never knew about this. She whispered to me that now I was going to be a big girl on whom she was going to have to depend, that this would happen every month. But most important, she told me, in Belgium and France, where we were heading, they had excellent napkins, much better than in Poland.

—Nina Bassman, Queens, NY

Nina taught French in a New York City public school and made the best beef brisket in the world.

The Artist, 1968

I think I was in the seventh grade. I had moved from a private school (class of twelve) to a public school (class of four hundred)—a big change—and had just cut off my braids and gotten my first bra. In class one day, I stood up, and my skirt stuck to me. I twisted around and saw a bloodstain on my tan corduroy skirt. It was only as big as a fifty-cent piece, but it seemed huge to me. Quickly I twisted my skirt around to the front and with my ballpoint pen colored in the spot. That was the official beginning of my career as an artist and the beginning of my staining many, many things: upholstered Louis XIV chairs at the Ritz-Carlton in London and a myriad of mattresses around the world, not to mention most of my clothes. And even though my period was regular almost to the day each month for about forty years, it always came as a surprise. I was never prepared. And with about nine pregnancies, when the doctor asked, "And when was your last period?" I never ever knew.

—Nina Bentley, Westport, CT

Nina is a visual artist whose work often deals with women's social issues. Her sculpture Corporate Wife . . . Service Award Bracelet *is part of the permanent collection of the New Britain Museum of American Art.*

Bloody Bat Mitzvah, 2002

I was not going to be caught off guard. I first read Judy Blume's book *Just as Long as We're Together* when I was about eleven. In it, the main character gets her period on her thirteenth birthday. From then on, I was constantly prepared to get my period when it was least expected. Would it be at camp? The first day of sixth grade? On vacation? I was prepared for the worst, the randomest, the least expected time.

When I was twelve and three months, I had my bat mitzvah. It was a whirlwind of a day—I was performing in front of all my family and friends and being welcomed into my Jewish community as an adult. When I got home from the main event, I was exhausted, and all I wanted to do was take a nap before the party that evening. I went into my room to change and use the bathroom. It turned out that at some point during my Hebrew chanting, I had become a woman all over my underwear. Although I had been attempting to expect the unexpected, I was truly not prepared for this one. Who gets their first period on the day of their bat mitzvah? What kind of a sick joke is that? I went into my mom's room and told her, exhausted and overwhelmed, "I think I just got my period." She responded, "Mazel tov!" My biggest fear was that she would go down into the living room filled with my extended family and announce to them the wonderful news: Sarah became a woman twice! Thankfully she didn't, but once I became a little bit more of a woman, I didn't mind sharing the story of my bloody bat mitzvah.

—Sarah Rosen, New Haven, CT

Sarah is an undergraduate at Yale. She does theater and somehow always ends up being cast as the ingénue.

Going to X-tremes, 1982

When I first sat down to write this, I was staggered to realize I didn't remember my first period. At all. Initially I thought maybe it had been *soooooooo* traumatic that I blocked it out, but that didn't seem right. Still, it left me in kind of a lurch for what to write about, so I asked a bunch of friends to tell me about their first periods, hoping I could make a story up based on one of their experiences—I mean, spur my memory. But something else happened instead. Listening to them, I discovered that how you react to Your First Period lets you see the beginnings of personality traits that are magnified as an adult. It gives a boldfaced glimpse of the behavior patterns you'll rely on later in life to make order out of a chaotic world.

So one friend, who is now the most independent and stoic person I know, got her period and wouldn't tell anyone but figured out how to deal with it without asking for help. Another friend who today can't decide if her favorite appliance is her paper shredder or her Roomba and lives on the Very side of Compulsively Tidy Street remembers her reaction to her first period was dismay because it was so *messy*. My friend who diagnoses herself with every disease she sees featured in an "Ask Your Doctor About . . ." ad on cable TV decided—despite having learned all about Getting It at school and from her mom—that she was dying and composed several very moving poem-plus-illustration combinations for her tombstone.

And then there was me.

From about the age of seven on, I'd been obsessed with feminine hygiene products. I surreptitiously snuck the instructions out of tampon boxes I found under the sink in my friends' parents' bathrooms; I pored over ads for tampons and pads in my mom's *Ms.* magazine; I haunted the Female Needs aisle of drugstores, saving my allowance to buy one of everything so I could develop strong opinions about scented or unscented, which applicator or shape was best, why all the major brands ended in X. In secret I puzzled over the "New! Beltless!" stickers on maxi pad packages, wondering where the belt previously could have gone. (Later I experienced what a treasure hunter, stumbling unexpectedly across a fabulous gold idol, must feel when I discovered, in a friend's grandmother's attic, a dusty box of *belted* maxi pads.) I was a feminine products archaeologist, a connoisseur of the $-X$ category of products. I was ready. By the time My First Period came, it was a nonevent, so much less exciting than the purchasing that led up to it.

In other words, I handled my first period all those years ago the way it turns out I handle most challenges: I shopped for it until I had the perfect thing to wear.

—Michele Jaffe, Los Angeles, CA

Michele is the author of a historical romance novel series about the Renaissance and of the YA hit Bad Kitty, *which recounts the adventures of a sleuthing teenager and her three-legged cat. Her hobbies include taco-eating, sparkly-shoe-wearing, and as her story reveals, shopping.*

blood relative, 1976

27

stories of intimacy
are in the details—
the nuance of connection
the way fondness translates into
a look, a nod, a smile.

i cannot remember any of these in our story.

my recollection is bare minimum,
a small pile of
bleached white bones.

the first time
i saw blood
come from between my legs
i yelled
from the bathroom,

clenching the gold shag rug
with my toes,
"mom!"

you replied, "here"
pushing a slender white cylinder
underneath the door
without opening it.

—Sondra Freundlich-Hall, San Francisco, CA

Sondra lives with her husband, Alan, and two sons, Jasper and Nico. She has been writing poetry since before she got her first period and hopes to continue writing it well beyond her last.

Too Wet, 1994

It was the summer after fourth grade. I was looking forward to going back to Jackson Road Elementary to finish off elementary school and get into the big leagues (White Oak Middle). At Jackson Road, I was, of course, the tallest girl in the class as well as the most developed. I was already wearing a real bra and beginning to have real crushes on boys. I had already begun to masturbate.

One afternoon, I noticed that I was feeling a little too wet and went to the bathroom to check things out. I was home alone with my older sisters, who were going through puberty problems of their own. I saw the bloodstain on my underwear and was frightened.

I wrapped up tissue and put it in a new pair of underwear. I washed out the dirty pair, hoping that no one would notice the stain. I had no idea what this red stuff was, and I was convinced that I had masturbated myself into a hemorrhage of some sort. But what was I going to tell my mom? That I was masturbating? I figured I would wait a couple of days to see if the blood would go away. Of course, it didn't.

By the third day, I was scared to death. I knew I had to tell my mother something. Tissue was not going to work forever. I began to cry. I called my mother at work.

"Mom? You know that place that you said maybe I would shave one day? Well, there's blood coming out of there!"

She began to laugh. As I was crying hysterically, I was convinced that my mother was enjoying the fact that I was dying.

"It's just your period, Rafia. It's okay. We will get you some pads. Talk to your sisters and tell them what happened."

And so I did. My older sisters and I had the period talk. When all was said and done, I no longer thought I was going to die. I realized that I had just been initiated into the wonderful world of puberty, and I learned to be grateful.

—Rafia

Rafia is a graduate student pursuing her interests in African health.

Guatemala: Advice from a Cheesemaker, 1953

I got my period late, around fifteen years old. My parents never said anything to me about it, because people just don't talk about those things. But a woman would come to our house to make cheese, and I liked to talk to her and watch how she did it. She talked to me a lot, and she was the one who told me what to expect. I had horrible cramps when I got my period, and she had warned me that it felt as painful as giving birth. My friend's parents had a pharmacy, and they gave me some pills to make the pain go away. We used towels to soak up the blood, because we didn't have the kinds of things you have here in America. It was very important not to eat anything "cold"—like avocado, cream, and other fresh foods—because this would make you worse, since you are in a hot state when you get your period. If you eat cold things, it will make your stomach swell and hurt even more. Also you're not supposed to eat eggs, because they say that this makes your menstrual blood smell bad. They also tell you not to bathe for three days, because they say this will make your veins pop out, but I think that's not sanitary.

—Flori, Chicago, IL

Flori is originally from a small town in southern Guatemala. She has four children.

Editor's Note: Theories of hot and cold are pervasive throughout Latin America, where women try to balance hot and cold states of being with foods, herbs, and medicines to which they ascribe hot and cold properties.

Mehn-su, 1992

I looked down and saw a small stain on my cartoon-printed underwear. Panic rushed over my body. I yanked up my pajama bottoms and sprinted toward my *unie's* room for help. I stopped at her door, waited for her to look up, and said in a small, scared voice, "Unie? Something's wrong."

At ten years old, I didn't know what it meant to have a period. The year before I started my period, in fourth grade, the girls had a day of "Sexual Health Education." My parents checked the "NO, I do not consent" box on my form. My parents grew up after the Korean War, when there was certainly no such thing as sex ed. The letter from my elementary school explained the purpose of sex ed, but my parents spoke limited English and they only needed to understand one word: *sex*. So, while all the girls learned about periods, pads, and puberty, I sat with the boys and watched *Big Ben*, a movie about a brown bear.

The morning that my period first started, my sister handed me one of my mom's bulgy pads and showed me how to use it. I secretly wondered why there was no "belt," as my only exposure to periods and pads was from an outdated version of *Are You There God? It's Me, Margaret,* in which Margaret and her friends yearn for their periods and practice fastening belts to a pad. I used pads every day for three weeks. I didn't know when it would come back and if I was supposed to wear pads just in case. I didn't know how to take a shower. I would rush out of the shower and put on my underwear as quickly as I could because I was scared that the blood would come gushing out. This was my introduction to my period: many questions and no answers.

My mother didn't find out that I had started my period until three days later. I didn't know how to say "period" in Korean. She asked me if I had started my *mehn-su.* I had no idea what *mehn-su* meant, but from my mom's tone, I could guess that she was talking about my period. I slowly nodded my head and she yelled in exasperation, "You're so young! Why are you starting so soon?!" I clearly did not have the answer to her question, so I silently added it to my list.

It wasn't until sixth grade, when I slyly moved the check mark from the NO box to the YES box, that I finally got some answers.

—Amy H. Lee, Berkeley, CA

Amy is a social justice educator in the San Francisco Bay Area.

Can I Just Skip This Period? 1971

I got my first period when I was almost sixteen. You might think that my long-drawn-out immaturity would have been embarrassing to me, but the opposite was true. I never believed that menstruation would be the beautiful experience described in *Becoming a Woman,* the booklet we fifth-grade girls received one afternoon when the boys were doing something fun, like pummeling each other on the recess blacktop. For a long time, I honestly felt that I was going to be the single female in all of history lucky enough to skip that aspect of adulthood altogether. When I discovered that I had gotten my period, I stomped into my mother's bathroom, where she was taking a shower.

"Guess what I got?" I roared petulantly to make myself heard above the water.

"What?"

"My period!"

"I think you're supposed to be happy."

"Well, I'm not!"

My mother told me that there were Kotex pads in her bathroom cabinet and asked me if I needed instruction. I told her I'd figure it out by myself, and I did.

I know you're thinking I should see a psychiatrist. You're probably right.

—Patty Marx, New York, NY

Patty Marx is a writer whose work appears regularly in the New Yorker. *She is the coauthor of many books, including* Meet My Staff, Now I Never Will Leave the Dinner Table, Now Everybody Really Hates Me, *and* How to Survive Junior High.

Silence, 1930s

In our days, talk about personal, intimate aspects of one's life was taboo. We didn't even talk of it to our own mother. We kept silent, timid, frightened, wondering what had happened. Among our girlfriends—they were even silent. It was as though our bodies gave us a punishment. Our ethnic background, too, helped to promote the silence. After so many years, I can still envision the agitation and the fear of becoming a woman. Thank God times have changed.

—Elizabeth Siciliano, Cleveland, OH

Elizabeth Siciliano is originally from Calabria, Italy. Her family never discussed anything having to do with the female body—from periods to pregnancy. She has two sons, five grandchildren, and four great-grandchildren.

A Jealous Vajayjay, 1981

Spring, 1981

My name is Nancy and I am the older sister. In 1981, I was fourteen, and my younger sister, Janet, was thirteen. Most of my friends were waiting for, or already had gotten, their periods. I was waiting to get mine, and I was prepared.

One afternoon, as I was sitting in the den watching *General Hospital* and eating Doritos, my parents' phone line rang. I answered it only to find my baby sister Janet crying into the phone.

"Nancy, I need your help," she said.

Bitchy older sister that I was, I replied, "What, what do you need?"

"I got my period!" Janet blurted out.

I could not believe it—my younger sister got her period before *me*!

"Are you kidding? I don't know what to do since I haven't gotten mine yet." With that, I nicely slammed the phone down.

In hindsight, how unthoughtful of me not to be a good big sister to Janet, but I was mad. I was supposed to get my period before her! This was a rite of passage, a coming of age if you will, and there I was sitting and stewing because my younger sister was blessed to have her vajayjay christened before me.

As my mother strode in from work that afternoon, Janet broke the news to her in a hesitant and wary fashion. My mother was actually quite stunned but very excited for Janet. Great, a party for her!

At the family dinner table that evening, I pouted, not even speaking to Janet, since of course it was her fault, not mother nature's!

My father, who was not a man of too many words during mealtime, blurted out to Janet, "So, I hear you became a woman today," and gave her an atta-girl pat on the back.

I freaked out and started crying hysterically. "Oh my God, are we going to make this a big deal at the dinner table?"

My mother gave my father "the look," while Janet, obviously embarrassed, sat with her head down and sullen. My seventeen-year-old brother looked around and put his napkin on the dining table, said, "Oh man, I'm outta here," and bolted from the room. Following suit, I, too, left the table in disgust, while my mother and father stayed there bickering over what appropriate dinner conversation really was.

Janet still sat there, stunned and utterly confused.

Needless to say, Janet eventually figured out what it meant to have her period, and she became the resident expert.

SUMMER 1981

It was the last day of ninth grade for me, and I was wearing my pale yellow fatigue pants. I went to the bathroom and, lo and behold, there was a red spot on my underpants! I finally got my period, great—right before summer and swimsuits! Naturally I had leaked onto my pale yellow pants and sat waiting in the bathroom until someone I knew entered and I was able to beg for assistance.

I ended up having to cover my butt with my Mead history binder.

As I skipped off the school bus into our driveway and through the garage door, I ran into the kitchen and greeted my mother giddily with my news. She was glad for me that I finally had my vajayjay day and commented, "Great, honey bunch, you should talk to Janet about this. She'll help you out and tell you what to do." How humiliating it was that I had to ask my younger sister what to do with my first period!

Little did I know at the time how much guidance I actually did need.

I went upstairs and told Janet my news. She was rather blasé about it and told me to grab a Tampax in the bathroom. Tampon in hand, I went back to Janet's bedroom and said to her quizzically, "Okay, what do I do with it?"

She looked at me as if I were stupid. "You just put it up inside you. That's what you do."

I looked back at her and replied with a not-knowing look, "The whole thing, just put the whole thing up inside me?" Janet replied, "Yeah, jeez."

HOW TO MAKE YOUR OLDER SISTER FEEL REALLY STUPID

So I went into the bathroom and took off my underpants, unwrapped the Tampax, and slowly put the whole thing up inside me. The whole thing—cardboard applicator and all. I didn't know there was such a thing as an applicator; no one had cared to tell me that part. Nonetheless, not all of it was inside me, about a quarter of it was peeking out, and as I'm sure you can gather, this wasn't very comfortable. I came walking out of the bathroom and into Janet's room, where she had been joined by my mother. I looked at them with disgust and exclaimed, "I don't think I did this the right way."

My mom and Janet both looked at me and replied, "Why, what did you do?"

I replied, "Well, I put it all up inside me, that's for sure. The whole thing. The cardboard isn't very comfortable, though."

Janet and my mom started laughing hysterically. Janet said, "You did what? You're not supposed to put the cardboard inside you; that's the applicator that holds the *tampon*!"

I still use Tampax mostly during my menstrual cycle now, but I do, from time to time, prefer a pad; there's less cardboard.

—Nancy L. Caruso, Cardiff, CA

Nancy is a part-time writer and full-time recruiting consultant.

Into the Woods, 1964

My wonderful mystery of life started during my tenth summer. Lucky me.

I was away at summer camp for the first time in my life, and of course that's when it had to start, when I was away from my mother, my friends, and even that funny little kit with the belts and different-sized pads and informative little booklets that my mother had stashed away in a drawer for my sister. She was older, so naturally they thought she'd start first, but hey, I fooled 'em again. The only positive thing about the whole debacle was knowing how pissed my sister was going to be that I started first, like there was anything I could do about it.

And of course, this was our night camping out in the woods—boys and girls together, thank you very much—and it came in the middle of the night with the bloated stomach and the cramps and the feeling that I had to poop, but of course I didn't because the pressure was coming from somewhere else. Actually, that's how I discovered it. I thought I had to go so bad that I finally decided it was more important to get up and put my sandals on and stumble across that stubbly field to the outhouse in the pitch black. It's a wonder I didn't step on anyone, but fortunately I didn't. The outhouse had a little tiny night-light kind of thing with a gazillion bugs buzzing around it. It gave just enough light for me to see the mess my pants were in, and I hadn't the faintest idea what to do about it. At least I knew what it was, thanks to that annoying *Girl to Woman* film they showed us in school every year and my mother's willingness to answer my questions.

That didn't help me much, though.

Finally I just put a giant wad of toilet paper in my pants and stayed awake all night so I could keep going back to the toilet to change the paper. My jeans were uncomfortable but at least dark enough that the blood didn't stand out. I didn't know what I was going to do with those underpants, though. They were ruined. I thought about burying them out there in the woods, but I knew I'd feel pretty stupid when the wild bears and mountain lions and hyenas dug them up and started fighting over them.

Fortunately, camp was over the next day, and my parents came to take me home. I told my mother about my predicament, and she sorted it all out. And when we got home, sure enough, I started in with the belts and pads from my sister's kit.

—Sharon Gerhard, Novato, CA

After twenty years of film production, Sharon has started a second career as a professional writer. She has written and published fiction, movie and travel articles, poetry, and screenplays. Her mother's story appears on page 69.

Loss and Gain of Responsibility, 1969

My first memory of my big day is marked by my dad's congratulations on my passage into womanhood. My mother had told him about the arrival of my period, just as she had done for my older sister two years earlier. I remembered my sister's disgust that my mother needed to share this event with my dad. In this summer of my twelfth year, I was experiencing that same feeling of being exposed and having more responsibility for myself. I nevertheless had a lot of good feelings because my mom had prepared me for this arrival.

Although my mother was a librarian by training, at the time of my first period, she was a stay-at-home mom. During my growing-up years, my mom practiced her library skills, such as her love of reading and the sharing of information, with her family and many of my friends. She gave my sister and me loads of books about menstruation, coming of age, female sexuality, and emotions years before our big day. Many of our friends would come over to our house to talk with my mom about their big day and growing-up issues. My friends felt uncomfortable discussing these topics with their own moms and knew we had a lot of information on the subject. She would always tell them to let their moms know that we were having these chats and that, if a mother considered this information inappropriate for her daughter to hear, she should let my mother know. Our friends' moms saw my mother as a credible and supportive resource and found it okay that she was having these chats with their daughters.

She would tell us stories of how black women came of age during the Depression and earlier in Virginia. She was brought up by her grandmother, who was born and reared in an enslaved African family in Virginia. Grandma was a young girl when her family was emancipated. My mother described how black women used cloths during this early time because disposable sanitary napkins were not readily available. Women had to go through a painstaking process to take care of themselves during their monthly periods. My mother also relayed stories from her grandmother about black women who had their first periods in Virginia during slavery. When these girls got their first period, it meant that they were now able to breed and suckle for their masters. It also meant that the young women lost the responsibility for their own bodies, feelings, and futures. Once these young women had their first period, they were often sold away from their families because they had become more valuable to their owners. The girls could be sold or hired out to other plantations for breeding or suckling duties. With the arrival of their first period, many of these young women were initially bred with their masters, members of his family, or other slaves on the plantation before they were hired out or sold to another plantation.

My mother always made us aware that as black girls, our first period was one of the most significant events in our lives. We were now capable of becoming mothers and needed to become more responsible for our bodies, our feelings and, in many ways, our futures.

On my big day, when my dad arrived with his well wishes, I was prepared for receiving them on many levels, though not for such a deep feeling of personal change. I knew when Dad congratulated me that I was no longer his little girl but a young woman. The carefree sense about myself, my body, and my life was over, and now I was responsible.

—Zannette Lewis, Richmond, VA

Zannette is a compensation and diversity consultant and an astrologist.

The Ming Period, 1999

There are periods of world history—large, expansive, extremely important and eventful times in human existence—that I will never remember, yet for as long as I live, I won't forget the Ming Dynasty, for it was to the noise of its soldiers' clashing swords that I became a woman. I was in seventh grade, age thirteen, and we were watching a movie on Chinese history. While the Mings were in the midst of expelling the Mongols, I began to feel this unearthly pain in my lower abdomen.

We were all sitting on the floor of the classroom to watch the movie, and I remember attempting to discreetly lie on my belly in hopes that it might go away. Facedown on the scratchy carpet, I tried to figure out was happening to me. My two guesses were (1) appendicitis and (2) my period. As the Mings were reforming the Chinese civil service examinations, I weighed my options. If it was appendicitis, then I would either have to go to the hospital or just die, and I would not have to come back to school in either instance. Of course, if I had gotten my period, then that was another matter—that meant a lot more.

Back in the days of middle school, at least at my middle school, getting one's period was akin to a competitive sport. Everyone knew who had theirs already; everyone couldn't wait to join the ranks of womanhood. My best friend at the time, whom I had known since preschool, had gotten hers a couple months earlier, and I remember sitting jealously in my living room as my mother congratulated her and explained to her about womanhood, what it meant to grow up, and the finer points of the tampon-versus-pad debate.

I was very excited, lying there on the carpet, at the notion that now it might be my turn. I ended up sticking it out for the whole film, which I still feel is quite an accomplishment—it was a very long movie; there is a lot that happened in fourteenth-century China. After a trip to the girls' bathroom and a harrowing experience with the pad dispenser, I got on the school bus to go home, excited to tell my mother the news. I expected a lot from that talk. I expected secrets to be revealed, meanings to be exposed, and to emerge somehow closer to my mother and her adult world. I remember beaming as she sat me down on her bed with a package of pads and launched into a similar version of the talk she had given my friend. But about five or ten minutes into it, her then-boyfriend got home from work and walked into the bedroom. She looked at me, handed me the package, and nothing more was said. My first period remained an event shared only by the Mings and me.

—Aliza Shvarts, Los Angeles, CA

Aliza Shvarts is a recent Yale graduate who double-majored in English and art. She is a conceptual artist whose projects have explored the philosophy of sexuality and the female body (including menstruation).

Andy Roddick's Serve, 2003

I was thirteen and at the U.S. Open (tennis) in New York with a friend and his family (only men). We were frying in the thirtieth row of Arthur Ashe Stadium when I felt something odd splurt out of me in the middle of Andy Roddick's serve. I waited in the long line to use the bathroom, the splurting now becoming more like a babbling brook. I finally made it to a stall, where I discovered I was spouting blood from my you-know-what. I cleaned myself up, but my shorts had acquired a lovely and rather large stain. I put the U.S. Open program around my butt and went out to the sink, scanning the women's faces. I dropped my program, and an elderly woman at the sink next to me said something along the lines of, "Hello, dearie, do you know that you've got blood on your shorts?" After buying new shorts from the gift shop, making a temporary toilet-paper diaper, and crying like a baby, I went back to my seat. I made frequent bathroom trips to reupholster my diaper, and we *finally* left. Of course, he and his family were dying of heat and thought that a quick swim at the country club after the hour-long drive would be *perfect*. Sweating bullets and crossing my legs, I watched my friend run up to the pool gate at the club . . . and the gate wouldn't open. The club was closed! Huzzah! When I got home, I didn't tell my mom until things got nasty in the middle of the night, when she explained to me that I was normal and not on the brink of death.

—Jen Bashian, Los Angeles, CA

Jen is an undergraduate at the University of Southern California. She insists that her story is ten times better when she can embellish it with gesticulations and impressions and can make faces and noises. She is an actress at heart.

An Invisible Period, 1981

I was a bit on the young side when I got it—maybe eleven—which is why I had not been told about it beforehand. I felt that I had suddenly lost control of my urinary tract. I couldn't understand why no matter how many times I went to the restroom, it kept coming. Finally, my mother noticed my stained clothes (despite my desperate attempts to hold it in) and pulled me aside and showed me how to use a sanitary napkin.

—S., New York, NY

S. has been blind since birth.

Oh, the "Joy" of Menses! 1987

Like many of my generation, the first time I ever heard anything about menstruation was when I read *Are You There*

God? It's Me, Margaret. I was only in third grade, a voracious reader who had already zipped through all the age-appropriate books in the Blume canon, so it's no surprise that I didn't get my facts straight. The most glaring error was how I thought my period was something I'd only get once in my life. When the bleeding stopped, it was over and done with forever, much like the period at the end of a sentence.

My punctuation-based misunderstanding was cleared up one summer afternoon two years later. My mom took me across the street to my best friend Adrienne's house to watch a very special film borrowed from the local middle school. It was this primitive form of audiovisual infotainment that taught me all about menarche and how it would open the door to the *wonderful world of womanhood*. I remember a soft-rock sound track and a lot of golden, backlit shots of long-haired teenage girls smiling, laughing, or gazing dreamily into the distance, all ostensibly overtaken by the joys of menses. It was, perhaps, the most boring series of images that have ever been committed to celluloid.

And yet, it had the desired effect on my best friend: Adrienne couldn't wait to buy—ew!—tampons. But I was more skeptical. Tampons were out of the question because I was afraid they could somehow break free from the vaginal canal and float around my body until I died of toxic shock syndrome. More troubling was the discovery that getting my period wasn't a one-shot deal after all and that I had *decades* of maxi pads ahead of me. Even in my unformed, prefeminist mind, this seemed like an inequitable proposition. Guys get "erections" (boners!) and have "nocturnal emissions" (wet dreams! So *that's* what was going on in Judy Blume's *Then Again, Maybe I Won't*). Girls bleed for a week every twenty-eight to thirty days until we're practically dead? *So* unfair.

But there was nothing I could do to stop the crimson tide. So for the next two years I watched my underwear, waiting for the blood to begin. At first I was so paranoid of being caught off guard that I packed "precautionary pads" in my knapsack, cleverly disguised as aluminum foil-wrapped perishables. But as months and years passed, I—paradoxically—began to worry less about the surprise arrival of my first period. Perhaps I was more preoccupied with issues that were already front and center, and literally so, in the form of what I was certain were the most stubborn zits in the history of pubescence.

When I asked for a pass to the girls' room during a pre-algebra test on an ordinary winter Wednesday in seventh grade, I wasn't expecting any life-changing thing to happen inside the stall. I was merely looking for some privacy so I could calm myself out of a sweaty, gut-churning panic over the realization that I had studied all the wrong formulas. But when I sat on the toilet and saw the muddy smudge in my underpants, I instantly recognized it for what it was. And I breathed a huge sigh of relief.

But I wasn't overcome by the joys of menses like the hippie girls in the film, oh no. I was grateful because I could go back to my math class and—with a telling raise of the eyebrows—silently explain to my (male) teacher that I had to go to the nurse right away for "feminine reasons." My mom would pick me up at school and take me out to McDonald's for a celebratory woman-to-woman lunch. And when I got home, I would be able to study for the test I would otherwise have failed. Maybe there was something to this period stuff after all.

It certainly wasn't the most enlightened epiphany or one that fully embraced my embarkation on the journey through the *wonderful world of womanhood*. But at least I didn't envy the boys anymore. After all, an erection would never get a guy out of a math test.

—Megan McCafferty, Princeton, NJ

Megan is the New York Times *best-selling author of the Jessica Darling series.*

The Blusher, 2002

Ever since all the girls in my fourth-grade class were exposed to an enormous picture of a vagina with a tampon in it, I'd been terrified of getting my period. That was also the class where they showed us what a uterus looked like, using pancake batter. I was so concerned that I actually raised my hand and asked whether or not I would still get my period if I walked on my hands for the rest of my life.

I didn't get my period until two years later. I was at

home, which was fine. Except that the only person at home was my father. And my father is a blusher. He doesn't talk about anything to do with sex at all, so I had to ask him where my mom kept the pads. And he didn't know because she didn't keep pads—she kept tampons.

I asked him to explain to me how tampons worked, but he was so embarrassed that instead he drove me to the pharmacy and we picked up a box of pads. I had basketball practice right afterward and we had to drive up together, as he was my coach. The forty-five-minute ride was spent in silence. When we finally got there, I blurted out, "It's just my period; it's not that big of a deal!" And he just blushed.

When, in the middle of practice, I started leaking because the pad was soaking through, one girl offered me a tampon, but I had to tell her I didn't know how to use one, and instead made one of those awkward makeshift pads with paper towels. If only I had paid more attention to the pancake-batter uterus. . . .

—Elli Foster, Lancaster, PA

Elli Foster is an undergraduate at Franklin and Marshall College. She is a top-twenty squash player in the U.S. nineteen-and-under division. She also loves to sing and directed her high school's gospel choir and a cappella group. She aspires to sing like Freddie Mercury and Aretha Franklin.

Hot Dog on a String, 1993

My own first-period story was unremarkable. I was twelve, and when I discovered its arrival, I walked downstairs to alert my mother. She was cleaning the litter box. She asked me if I was sure that I had actually begun to menstruate. I detested the word "menstruate" and considered lying about it and going back up to my room just to avoid hearing or using the word again, but instead, I said I was sure. After being subjected to countless hour-long "girls-only" presentations made by the school nurse, as she explained the "special" change our bodies would go through, I was fairly confident that I was undergoing the "magical process" that Nurse Joan had described in detail while the boys in my class got to play an extra game of kickball. My mother finished her task of scooping hard clumps of litter into a plastic bag, dusted her hands off, and declared we would have to celebrate. Aside from the brief trauma of having to bear my mother's Coca-Cola toast honoring my development into womanhood while we dined on baked ziti, the event passed without great incident.

Far more notable was the first time I became aware of tampons. I was four years old and had developed a habit of sitting outside the bathroom on the second-floor landing as my mother went through her ablutions in preparation for the day. Tucked in a ball, snuggled into the corner, I would watch her walk from the shower, to the closet, to the sink. I was raised in a naked house. The bathroom door was always open, and we regularly walked unclothed to and from the shower. While this particular dynamic in my family would lead to moments of intense embarrassment as a teenager (my mother's proclivity for hand-washing dishes in the buff, for instance, was a source of tremendous secret shame throughout my high school career), as a young girl, I cherished the opportunity to quietly watch my mother in her morning ritual. While sitting, unobserved, in my corner, I would also watch my mother use the toilet.

Aside from the juvenile delight I took in hearing urine hit the surface of toilet water and the endless hilarity inherent in the gentle tearing sound of farts, my mother's routine was so dear to me because it represented the complete intimacy of our relationship. I knew what her bare feet sounded like as they padded across the tile floor; I knew just where her sun-exposed, freckle-filled skin gave way to smooth, white paleness; I knew exactly how her soft flesh folded over the scar that split her abdomen in two. I knew her completely and I loved her.

In my child's notion of time, it seemed to me that I had spent my whole life perched on that landing watching my mother. It was the disruption of this familiar eternity that made it all the more shocking when, one day, I saw her do something that she had never done before. Between moisturizing her legs and blow-drying her hair, my mother paused, placed her right foot upon the toilet seat, reached between her legs, and removed a hot dog on a string. My eyes grew wide as I watched the hot dog dangle from its small string while my mother wrapped it in a tissue and placed it on the counter. I involuntarily gagged, as I was overwhelmed with the sense that I had witnessed something I wasn't supposed to see. In my memory, I had never seen my mother do anything like this, so it opened up a world of questions. Why did my mother store hot dogs in her vagina? Did she always store one in there? Was she able to store more than one? Why did she take it out? What would she do with it now? Did other women keep hot dogs in their vaginas? Why did this hot dog have a string? I was too distracted by my own questions to notice my mother insert a fresh, white tampon moments later. Instead, my four-year-old brain was overrun by the multitude of questions the mystery of the hot dog had presented. A combination of confusion and shame forced me out of my viewing nook and into my bedroom. That sensation of confusion and shame only built as more and more questions occurred to me and as I became more and more resolved that I could not ask my mother for answers.

It was not the possibility that my mother might occasionally store foodstuffs in her lady parts that shook me. Hot dogs were ubiquitous in my childhood. As far as I could tell they were used for everything from meaty filler in macaroni and cheese to 3-D eyes and noses on the paper snowmen we made during craft time at day care. It was entirely conceivable that they might also be capable of serving some function in a vagina, though I had little sense of what functions a hot dog or a vagina might have.

Similarly, the concept of placing foreign objects into one's orifices was not unfamiliar, as I had a friend who delighted in sticking marbles in his nose. The source of my apprehension and the reason I felt so shaken was that my mother had inadvertently revealed that there was something I did not know about her. Despite my careful and regular observations, my mother maintained a secret from me. I had heard her contentedly sigh and grunt after a bowel movement dozens of times, but I had never seen this.

Clearly, it was a mystery that was meant to be kept a mystery, and I had violated some boundary by witnessing it.

My sense of unease, guilt, and curiosity lingered throughout the day. I considered investigating the cabinets, drawers, and garbage can of the bathroom in order to quiet the questions that persisted in their demands for answers, but my vague sense that some taboo had been broken kept me from doing so. What would I do if I found the hot dog? What would it mean? Would I even want to see it? Touch it? No.

There were too many uncertainties, and I was seeking to regain the stability and comfort I had always associated with my mother. Whatever mystery I had caught a glimpse of should not be explored or researched further.

My terror that I had unintentionally stumbled upon a sacred and secret rite was eventually eased. Two days later, I nearly forgot that it had happened as the joys of summer lured me off the second-floor landing and out into the back-yard. A few years later, I learned what tampons were, and a few years after that, I learned to use one myself. During all that time, the story of the hot dog on a string stayed in my memory, but I never told it to anyone.

The situation that I had believed was fraught with taboo and mystery was, in many ways, commonplace and benign. I had not disrupted the fabric of the universe, and I was not the accidental interloper. At the same time, on that day, sitting on that landing, I was part of a sacred rite—just not the one my overactive imagination had created. On that day, I learned that my mother was more than I knew her to be. Within her were mysteries that no number of open bathroom doors or dishes washed in the nude would ever reveal. And so, years before I would ever face the rite of passage of my own first period, I experienced a different rite. The discovery of my mother's menstruation revealed her as a full and complex woman to me. In that way, the hot dog on a string proved as sacred and mysterious as I had initially believed.

—Ellen Devine, Wallingford, CT

Ellen is a writer and a teacher of English at Choate Rosemary Hall. If she could relive her first period, she would have her mother be doing something besides scooping kitty litter.

Chairman Mao's Period, 1967

During the Cultural Revolution in China, toilet paper—the kind that comes in rolls—was tightly rationed. This was really discrimination against having girls. My family—with three girls—used to cope by taking the coarser brown paper towels, which were more readily available, and cutting them up in strips for everyday bathroom use, so as to save the toilet paper for us when we had our periods. Since I was the second oldest, I knew what to expect. But I was still anxious, because I knew the arrival of my period would put a strain on our supply of toilet paper.

At the time, having your period was still something to be kept completely secret. The day my period arrived, my family and I were scheduled to do our manual labor in a local park. We were to do planting, landscaping, and cleaning up. My parents offered to write a note to excuse me from my work, but I insisted that I go. I was so sure that such a note would instantly expose what was happening.

—Xiao Ling Ma, Nanjing, China

Xiao Ling Ma immigrated to the United States with her family in the aftermath of the Tiananmen Square massacre.

LOL {.}, 2005

Glittergrrrl007 (Lauren): Hi zoe!

Bananab0at (Me):   .

Glittergrrrl007: ???

Bananab0at: •

Glittergrrrl007: I don't get it . . .

Bananab0at: ➔ •

Glittergrrrl007: big red dot . . .

Bananab0at: What is this?   .

Glittergrrrl007: OMG did yu get ure period????

Bananab0at: Yea, I'm pissed

Glittergrrrl007: Join the club

Bananab0at: Guys are sooo lucky they don't get a period

Glittergrrrl007: Yea, but u no wat happens when a guy sees a hot girl . . .

Bananab0at: LOL

Glittergrrrl007: LOL

Bananab0at: Well only 40 more years 2 go!!

Glittergrrrl007: yea, LOL

BananaB0at: Well gtg, ttyl, tear

Glittergrrrl007: ok, by!

—Zoe Kauder Nalebuff, New Haven, CT

Zoe is a high school student whose interests include taxidermy and sculpture. Her first thought after getting her period wasn't where she could find a pad but that she would have to write down her story for her older sister.

Blood on the Tracks, 1972

My first period was a bittersweet event. Even at eleven, my best friend was plump and curvy enough that the boys in the neighborhood would ogle her breasts. In my skinny, little-girl body, I felt scrawny and insignificant by comparison. Then when she bragged that she got her period at twelve, I was even more envious. In the privacy of my bathroom, I'd look down at my pale, flat chest and wonder when—and if—all these mysterious, womanly things would happen to me.

The summer before I turned fourteen, my friend and I were caught in a rainstorm while walking along the brick streets of my Pittsburgh neighborhood. For that afternoon, our differences disappeared as we splashed through the dirty rainwater like little kids. We were having such fun, two muddy girls, giggling and hurling mud and water at one another! But because I was thirteen, I was also afraid that somebody I knew would see us acting so juvenile. When I got home and peeled off my muddy shorts and underwear, I noticed a stain that wasn't mud. I was relieved to see that I'd finally gotten my period. But I also felt sad to realize that someday soon, I would no longer be interested in playing in mud puddles. I now had to worry about sanitary napkins and those torturous instruments that held them in place and whether I'd be able to go swimming or even splashing in puddles.

Having periods became vastly more comfortable once I began to use tampons. And more recently, as a grown woman, I've discovered another use for these products. For my husband's fortieth birthday, I treated him to a Bob Dylan concert. We had great seats, but the music was far too loud. I poked around in my purse, looking for a tissue to plug my ears with. No luck. But there, at the bottom of my bag, lay two small, compact o.b. brand tampons. What the heck, I thought. It's dark, and I've got long hair. Yes, I did plug my ears with tampons. And yes, I did listen to the rest of the concert with a sanitary product in my ears. To this day, I have a hard time listening to *Blood on the Tracks* without laughing.

—Patricia E. Boyd, Pittsburgh, PA

Patty is a freelance editor and weekend soccer warrior. She lives with her husband and two sons. She believes that we owe our ears the same protection that we owe our underwear and therefore recommends using tampons as earplugs.

Ink Blots and Milk Spots, 1987

When it comes to childhood, my childhood, it is difficult—impossible even—to negotiate the boundaries between what really took place, what I dreamed, what I dreamt up, what was read, what I wrote. All my memory can do is attempt to cobble together some of the images that haunt, put words to this ineffable space where fiction meets nonfiction, this place also known as life.

I've been shot! I screamed, more to myself than out loud. When I awoke one morning in the twin bed of my adolescence, I noticed that my T-shirt and gray sweatpants were wet with haphazard dark spots, as if riddled with bullets. I had been dreaming that I was Joan of Arc of shaved head about to be killed, only they had given me a pick of poisons. I chose firing squad over guillotine. Not the head; please, sirs, anything but the head.

After a few heart-racing seconds of delirious panic, I found the culprit. There was a felt-tip pen in my bed, uncapped, and I must have fallen asleep mid-diary entry, rolled around with it in some contorted dance, making a bloody mess of everything in the night—the ink spreading through the paper, my clothes. The sheets even bore signs of a pen's oozing wounds.

At Saturday's ritual pile of pancakes, no one noticed the black ink on my lip.

"I've been eating ink," I told them regardless.

A little taste of what was to come.

Eighth grade, tangled time of trying too hard. Fell up the stairs in my gray high heels, clutching my pile of schoolbooks to my forever-concave chest. Wore a miniskirt one day to win the attention of David, my since-second-grade crush. Only it was cold and I was blue with goose bumps, and he laughed at the prickly texture of my legs. Another day and I was white, all white. I was wearing an ankle-length blousy white skirt, white flats, white buttoned shirt. All the better to see stains on, apparently.

"You have chocolate milk or something on the back of your skirt," someone said on the way out from the lunchroom. Figures, I must have sat in some. My practical inclination was to simply rotate the skirt, back to front, and let the stain sit where I could at least claim ownership and try to protect it in the pleats of my lap.

The second I stepped onto my front lawn I always had to hurry to the toilet, the conditioned sight of mere grass daily triggering the need to pee. I ran inside into the urine-yellow tiled bathroom my brother and I shared and tugged my underwear to my knees. In midrelease, I noticed this rust-colored crust on the central strip of my panties. Not chocolate. I guess I knew what it was, I couldn't have not, and yet, some chosen confusion perhaps, and suddenly a need for:

"Mom! Quick! Come here!"

"What do you want? I'm trying to cook dinner," rising up from the furnace vents. Tuna casserole: that would take her hours, at least.

"Please! I need help!" Hoping an urgency of tone would compel her away from a boiling pot of macaroni.

"What's the matter?"

"There's something in my underwear!"

In minutes, a sucking sound as she pulled in her breath in the widening space between door and frame. She looked frightened, which frightened me. "The Curse; I think it's

61

here," she whispered in the direction of my muddy under-wear.

"What does that mean?"

"It means . . . it means . . . I . . . I take you to get your ears pierced." A pat on the back with her tentative hand. "Soak those in the sink with lukewarm water."

"My ears pierced?"

"Yes, well, that's what my mother did with me when I got my period."

"My per . . . what . . . ?"

Period. The end of the sentence. I must be dying, I thought. Death by dots.

No, that's not true, it didn't happen like that, did it? There was sex ed, there were books with terms, there was a mother and a mother's mother who must have at least pro-vided some subliminal hint of womanhood. And wasn't I excited? Finally, my ears pierced, I had my first earrings picked out for years, although they had since grown out of style. There was that word in the textbook, *menarche*, which sounded to me like the monarchs that flitted confetti-like over the raspberry patch. And there were the other bleeders. I would finally be joining their ranks. These bosom-since-birth girls with their ready-made boyfriends. It was a progression toward romance and motherhood, ma-turity and death, and I must have been excited, however frightened.

Best friend Brigit and Mom gathered outside the door of the basement bathroom, where I struggled within with this strange cardboard-wrapped cork. "Prop your leg up on the seat," they advised.

"I can't do it," I yelled back.

"Yes you can!" they cheered. "Just relax."

But my hands were nervous. My mom's super-plus had me nonplussed. It was a tad awkward, devirginizing yourself like this over the toilet. Tampons would have to wait.

Dad could measure the wingspan of a bald eagle flying a mile above, but he didn't notice—we both pretended not to notice—the soiled maxi pad that fell out of my loose pant leg and landed between our feet on the lawn. We both looked up as if to blame the sky for our embarrassment, this unspoken truth evidencing itself in the grass. And when I tried to give it a kick toward the mulch pile, the adhesive refused.

Menarche, pretty word for a difficult time, yet I return and return, writing it whenever I write something bigger, in every novel some scene in which I bleed, she bleeds, this character bleeds. I invent it anew, write it a different way, embellish, lie, and all in the interest of telling the truth.

—Krista Madsen, Brooklyn, NY

Krista is the author of the novels Degas Must Have Loved a Dancer *and* Four Corners *(Livingston Press), the mother of Kaia, and the founder of a Brooklyn wine bar called Stain (how appropriate!).*

Glamorous, but Not for Long, 1981

By the time I was in fifth grade (1980), I had read every book by Judy Blume I could get my hands on—including the famous *Forever . . .* , which taught me about premature ejaculation and Ralph, the penis of the protagonist's first lover. But the Blume book that meant the most to me (because it most closely mirrored where I was in life) was not *Forever . . .* , nor *Tales of a Fourth Grade Nothing*, but *Are You There God? It's Me, Margaret.* The "Ralph" scenes in *Margaret* had to do with getting your period—and I was obsessed with getting mine. By sixth grade, I would practice wearing mini pads, stolen from my mother's stash, in my underwear, and any time I had a stomach pain, I'd ask my parents if it might be cramps. "It might be," they'd say in earnest tones, thinking I was anxious to get it. Actually, the opposite was true—I wanted it as soon as possible. I think it equaled getting on with being grown up, which struck me as glamorous (I was already reading *Forever . . .* and, Barbies aside, was sick of kid's play) and also powerful— since being a child is to be dependent.

I finally got my period in sixth grade. I was at school when I went to the bathroom during sixth-period science class and saw the smear of brownish blood. I was a little surprised that the blood wasn't bright red, but other than that, I just felt excitement. I walked home, practicing how I would announce it to my mother. I remember almost getting hit by a car crossing the street, I was in such a proud reverie while walking home. I burst in the door, found my mom in the den, and said, "I got my period today," in a nonchalant way.

My older sister had gotten hers just months earlier, and I felt superior (or at least equal) that mine came when I was younger, since I believed the timing of your first period was somehow correlated with the timing of your glamorous adult life. My dad came home and so Mom told him, too—or maybe she suggested that I tell him. Either way, it was a little embarrassing, but I agreed he should be in on the big news.

The second day of my first period was exciting, too, as I told all of my friends. But after that, I can't say I loved getting it anymore, unless I was worried I was pregnant. Once I achieved that marker of womanhood, my period was revealed to be saddled with tedious chores. Having a time each month when the blood-rich lining of my uterus comes out of my body over the course of several days isn't awful, but it is extra work and preparation and sometimes a ruined pair of underpants or sheets. I'm always pretty relieved when it's over . . . though I wonder if I'll be relieved when it's really over. Is there a Judy Blume book that makes menopause glamorous yet?

—Jennifer Baumgardner, New York, NY

Jennifer is the author of Look Both Ways: Bisexual Politics *and* Abortion & Life *as well as the coauthor of* Manifesta *and* Grassroots. *She produced the documentary* I Had an Abortion *and is currently at work on a multimedia rape-awareness project called* I Was Raped. *She lives in Brooklyn with her son, Skuli.*

I Know You Are Not There, God. It's Me, Kate, 1990

I want to take a journey to a little place I know, a place filled with braces, rampant mall hair, and the inexplicable need to wear neon bicycle shorts. A place called Adolescence (here, circa 1988–1992). It is at this ugly, ugly time that many of us first experience that most bizarre of bodily functions, The Period. For me and several of my friends, it is also at this time that we discovered the yawning chasm between life as people say it is and life as it really is. There are many people to blame for this, but in my experience the makers of sex-education films and Judy Blume are the prime offenders.

Starting in grade four, I had to watch an ever-sillier parade of "health" filmstrips. The first one starred Marilla Cuthbert from *Anne of Green Gables* as a farmer whose horse was pregnant. Over the course of the film, the horse gets larger and crankier and eventually produces a baby horse, at which point everybody *oooohs* and *aaaahs* over the Miracle of Life, and flute music plays. The random children in the film ask Marilla/Farm Lady about the horse's pregnancy, and she answers in nonthreatening-yet-anatomically-detailed language. We were all pretty bored, having come to class prepared for hard-core porn (why else would they make our parents sign a permission form?). Afterward life carried on much the same as before, which is to say comfortably abstract. The next year, though, things started to get freaky. This time it was filmstrips from the early 1970s featuring the most hideously unattractive people the casting director could dig up, probably in a *Degrassi*-esque attempt to make us relate. The first featured a boy who was having some masturbation issues. (Mastur-what? Marilla, why hast thou forsaken me?) This velour-clad gent, whom we'll call Luke, lived in fear of growing hair on the palms of his hands, turning blind, etc., and in one Oscar-worthy scene, he had to secretly wash his sheets in the middle of the night after an "accident." The entertainment value is unparalleled, and the message is a good one: you're not a freak, don't believe your friends, and consider investing in rubber sheets. Fine. The final film, though, was the one that had the most resonance. It involved a girl we'll call Amy who was a paragon of well-adjusted girlhood. She was superproud of her "new breasts" (an actual quote that has stayed with me for the past fifteen years) and wore tight orange turtlenecks everywhere to show 'em off. One day she gets her period, much to her delight, and this completes her Voyage to Womanhood. The narrator seems really happy for her, too, rambling on about how much more attractive she is to boys and ain't it grand to be a lady. Gone is the "Yeah, puberty's kind of gross and creepy, but eventually it will seem funny" punch-on-the-arm approach of the boys' film. Now it's all about workin' it in an orange turtleneck at the seventh-grade dance. I'm not sure why girls were supposed to matter-of-factly accept their sudden status as sex objects with nary a whimper, but there it is.

This brings me to Judy Blume's novel *Are You There God? It's Me, Margaret*. If you haven't read it, it's about a girl named (wait for it . . .) Margaret who positively lusts for her period and goes so far as wearing a belt and pad around so that she will be prepared when the Day of Days finally comes. She's a bit like those doomsday prophets who wear the sandwich boards. Anyway, at last she gets her damned period and she's suddenly mature and content and somehow more, just like that. It's Amy all over again, sans the turtleneck (although Margaret does misguidedly fashion some "new breasts" out of cotton balls in an earlier episode, but I digress). It's as though these girls read the Secrets of Adulthood in their bloody drawers, tea-leaf style, and afterward they are unshakably chill. That's all fine and good, but if my life is at all typical, it is also a dirty stinkin' lie.

Contrasting adolescent Kate with Amy and Margaret is a dismal exercise indeed. In this blossoming-woman story, twelve-year-old Kate wakes up the day of her soccer tournament to discover that something is very, very wrong. Kate cries and must play The Big Game in what is essentially a diaper, and won't tell anyone for a year, including her best friend, in the hope that it will go back where it came from and the slate will be wiped clean. Kate is thoroughly convinced that she is a freak of nature since all her friends have also adopted the code of silence. Where is my sparkly glow of womanhood? Where is the pride and quiet confidence? It is nowhere.

Over the years that followed, I learned that none of my friends had managed to greet the momentous occasion with anything other than panic and horror. More than one of them assumed that they had suffered a bout of incontinence upon first getting their period, while others made doomed attempts to fashion pads out of Kleenex so as to avoid having to ask anyone for help. I don't think we could've believed Amy and Margaret even if we wanted to. Unlike Luke, any insecurity or fear they might have had is never discussed. I'm sure the filmmakers and Judy had only the best intentions, but they were also laboring under the early 1970s / flowing hair / Helen Reddy / Essential Woman paradigm that just didn't fly in 1989 suburbia. Being confronted with proof of one's womanhood in a misogynistic culture is a really scary thing.

—Kate Zieman, Toronto, Canada

Kate is a recovering academic, librarian, and cofounder of the queer indie press Homosaywhat? She thinks that first periods would be easier if we viewed them as one of the many steps toward adulthood instead of as automatic womanhood.

The Curse, 1939

I was eleven years old when I first got "The Curse," which was the slang term for the monthly period in 1939. I know, I know, it happens to every girl at some time in her youth.

The difference was in my surroundings. I lived in an orphanage, which was really an institution for boys and girls whose parents couldn't take care of their children and have a job at the same time, especially during the Depression. There were 125 children housed in six buildings, a mix of boys and girls. My first period arrived at the dinner table. I hadn't a clue as to what was happening. There I was, sitting at the table, same as always, except there was something wet running down my leg. I thought at first that one of the other kids had spilled milk. Nope. That wasn't it. I looked under the table and there near my chair was a little pool of blood. What was happening? What do I do now? We were supposed to ask permission to leave the table; I just got up and ran for the bathroom. Upstairs I went, stripped off my underpants, shoes, and socks, all covered with blood. Where did it come from? And how come?

Finally dinner was over and the housemother, Mrs. Riggs, came upstairs and rescued me. She took me into her apartment, helped me clean up, and handed me an oblong, gauze-covered cotton form. What was I supposed to do with this big bandage? She also handed me a narrow pink elastic belt that had two metal hooks equidistant on it. Now what? She told me to expect this once a month. That was it for sex education. I was told to talk to my mother about it on her next visit. In the meantime, Mrs. Riggs wrote a note of explanation for her. But more was to come. Whenever I needed more pads, I had to go to Mrs. Riggs for them, and she would give me four or five at a time. I used more than that every month. Part of the reason for this paucity was that we had very little private storage space. But mostly it was to keep it a secret from the other girls in the cottage who weren't "initiated" yet. Oh yes! We weren't to talk to any of the other girls about it. We had to keep it a "Big secret! Big surprise!"

—Lola Gerhard, San Francisco, CA

Lola and her younger sister went to live in an orphanage after her parents divorced. She spent the Depression and World War II there, along with more than a hundred other children. She has been married for fifty-five years and has four children, one of whom is a contributor. Her daughter Sharon's story appears on page 38.

The Simple Vase: Part I, 1997

The whole thing required, at least from my perspective, a series of readjustments. For instance, my friends and I had long wanted to make a special celebration for my daughter when she got her first period. We had articulated some lovely ideas about women and the moon and the tides, and we began discussing this ceremony when Rebecca was born. But as the time approached, it became unavoidably evident that the last thing a thirteen-year-old would want was to have to share this event with a bunch of her mother's middle-aged friends. Maybe in the abstract, in some other cultures, at some other time, but not in real-life Hamden, Connecticut, at the end of the twentieth century. What could I have been thinking?

Or, again, there was the day that I tried to talk with Rebecca about supplies and she showed me the kit they had long ago given her at school, looking at me as if I were just a complete loss. In retrospect I think that I might actually unconsciously have been trying not to be left behind. But in truth, I didn't stand a chance. It was one of life's great lessons.

Or even there was the day, years earlier, when a discussion about abortion came on the car radio and a five- or six-year-old Rebecca demanded an explanation of the term. Her horror at the idea that you could stop a baby from growing inside a mommy was searing and absolutely personal since, of course, it was the baby with whom she identified, and not the mommy. I learned that day never to assume what another female would think about the female body and the reproductive process—even a six-year-old one.

Probably she knew that when the event occurred, I would get all proud and excited, because her actual announcement was exceedingly casual. Rebecca got in the car and waited for me to drive her halfway home before happening to mention that she had gotten her period at school that day. But then, after just a couple of words of joy, I surprised myself as well as my daughter by suddenly turning into the parking lot of a flower shop we had almost passed. Beaming, and much to her embarrassment, I chose the first likely looking vase from a small display on a table, ordered it filled with a dozen red roses, and presented it to her right then and there, quite unceremoniously.

"Why are you giving me that?" she kept asking. The only thing I could think to answer was something like "Because you have to have it and I am so proud of you." She humored me most of the rest of the way home until I suggested that we put the vase and flowers on the dining room table, after which she took hold of it firmly and brought it right upstairs to her own room and forbade me to speak of it to anyone else. Of course, again!

So we never really discussed much outright about her getting her period, but the vase remained on her bureau all during junior high school and high school. The roses were long gone, and the vase came to hold things like ribbons and buttons, but it was always right there next to the mirror. Once in a while I would pick it up and look at it—it is a plain glass thing, a little thick and not really very pretty. Sometimes I would tell her I was sorry that I hadn't gotten her a much more elegant crystal vase, which I surely would have done if I had planned at all what I was doing. But she would say that I was silly. She didn't want a different, fancier vase—she wanted that one.

And so it went to college with her, where it stood on her bureau next to her mirror and where, if I am not mistaken, it occasionally held flowers given her by persons other than me.

—Laura Wexler, New Haven, CT

Laura is a professor of American studies at Yale.

The Simple Vase: Part II, 1997

I discuss everything with my mother, from details of a postal package to grand life plans. I spend far more time on the phone with her than with anyone else. So it surprised me to realize that until I read her essay about my first period, we hadn't really talked about the experience beyond the day it happened. I know I wanted it that way at the time, but it didn't occur to me that without further discussion, her memory of the event might prove so different from mine.

For example, I would not characterize her as being left behind, but as being ahead of the curve. While my thirteen-year-old self may have been horrified at the prospect of enduring a public period "outing" by my mother's friends, I took her enthusiasm to heart. I recall feelings of strength and pride during my first few periods. When some of my friends expressed negative emotions about their menstrual cycles, I would respond that mine made me feel tough and cool. Eventually I even organized my own moon and tide ceremony in which my high school friends and I frolicked in the woods late into the night before we crawled into sleeping bags and read about Rosh Hodesh from a book of feminist Jewish theology my mother gave me.

It's not that having a mother ahead of the curve was always easy. But in the end, I would say that my mother mixed forthright celebration of my womanhood with a fine-tuned sensitivity for my privacy. Indeed, in response to my lockdown of the roses, she gave me a small pair of silver earrings with a single flower and stem twisting into the shape of a heart. I have worn these earrings for years, a discreet and personal reminder of my mother's pride in my strength and development. They traveled with me to college, to England, and to New York, where they are sitting by my computer as I type. I imagine the flowers my mother gave me are right here beside me, fresh and enduring.

—Rebecca Wexler, New York, NY

Rebecca is a freelance documentary filmmaker.

Let Down, 2007

It was just a warning at first, a few dots of red that whispered a timid "Hello." While I suppose it was the kindest possible beginning, it was disappointing all the same. I wanted drama, meaning, and more blood than a teen horror flick. Yet there it was—a pair of spotted panties scrunched into a ball and thrown into the hamper.

My mother was screaming for me to come downstairs and help her get ready for the party, my party. She was marching up the stairs, banging on the door, but I was silent. She told me to grow up and come down; I was thirteen and acting like a child.

My voice returned only after she had wandered into the kitchen.

"Mom . . . *Mom? Moooooooooooom!!!!!*"

I couldn't go downstairs to tell her. I couldn't tell her in front of my brother and father. This had to be special, ritualistic, and tribal. In my little-girl mind, I was a woman.

She ignored me for fifteen minutes.

Finally she pounded on the door of the bathroom that had become my prison.

"Tatum! Hurry up! The cousins called and say they are on their way."

Red face.

Shaking hands.

Opened door.

"Come in . . . please?"

I whispered my secret.

She dug underneath the sink and with a shrug handed me a box of tissue-thin pads.

I was thoroughly let down.

—Tatum Travers, Chicago, IL

Tatum is a high school student who loves poetry and folk songs.

Desperately Delayed, 1970

As the youngest of four girls in my family, the event of the first period was a *big deal*. My passage through puberty took forever, it seemed, and my sisters were well ahead of me. I couldn't wait to develop some curves on my sticklike figure, but by age fourteen, my silhouette still drew a straight line from chin to toe, and my period had not yet come. Embarrassed at being such a late bloomer, I took to lying about my nonwomanly state.

Sex education in ninth-grade health class was taught by Miss Morgan, who had a large round nose, a sporty haircut, and beefy knees revealed by the short athletic kilts she wore to class. Following a brief lecture on the female reproductive organs, she launched into a description of menstruation and sanitary products, including tampons, which she mispronounced "tampoons," to our infinite delight. She next asked us all to raise our hands if we had begun having periods, and when I glanced around the room and saw that I was the only one with my hand down, mine shot up in a flash, foiling her attempt to point out that not all girls mature at the same time. There was no way I was letting her use me as the late-blooming poster child.

Miss Morgan also taught phys ed, and when a girl was having her period, she could be excused from showering after gym class if she quietly whispered "R" to Miss Morgan, who would mark her clipboard accordingly. What, I often asked myself, could the *R* possibly stand for—regular? ripe? red? After the white lie in health class, I felt compelled to sashay up to the clipboard occasionally, towel around my beanpole frame, and casually say, "R," while Miss Morgan peered over the rim of her glasses and gave me a skeptical look. Fortunately, she didn't humiliate me by blowing my cover.

When my period still hadn't come by age sixteen, I was desperate. Maybe I would never cross the threshold into adulthood. Maybe I would remain a girl forever. To bolster my spirits, my parents arranged an appointment with a gynecologist, who determined that I was just fine, but that perhaps my pituitary gland needed a jump-start. He suggested a brief trial of birth control pills to artificially stimulate my period, and thus eliminate my fears that I was missing some crucial piece of female plumbing.

Immensely relieved that a solution was at hand, I proceeded to the pharmacy with my understanding dad (no female secrets in this family). As we waited for the order to be filled, the two matronly women behind the counter exchanged openly disapproving glances. Barely able to disguise their contempt, they were outraged that this waif was getting birth control pills, and with her father's consent to boot. Or maybe they thought he was my very-much-older boyfriend. Who knew? I was furious. Here I was about to secure my coveted entry into the women's club, and these two harpies were ruining the moment.

"Dad," I said in a voice a bit louder than it needed to be as I snatched the prescription from the pharmacist, "I really hope this medicine helps to *regulate my period*." I turned on my heels and marched off, not even looking back to see how they took the news. I don't think my dad had a clue what was bugging me.

The pills performed as promised, and at last it was my turn to navigate the mysteries of the "tampoon," coached by my loving sister Pat from her discreet post outside the bathroom door.

After only one month on the pill, my body took over on its own, completing my prolonged but nonetheless joyful passage into womanhood.

—Judy Nicholson Asselin, Westtown, PA

Judy is a freelance writer and middle-school teacher.

Proper Disposal, 1993

Some years ago, when my daughter was thirteen, her best friend, Catelin, came for an overnight. During the night, for the first time, her period began. Fortunately, her mother had prepared her and she had a supply of pads. However, while her mom had done a great job describing what would happen, she had apparently been vague on the issue of used-pad disposal. As I made breakfast, my then-husband went into the bathroom and to his horror saw a large pad in the toilet! It had apparently been there for some time and had soaked up all the water in the bowl, so it was the size of a phone book. Frantically, he called for backup and fled to the garage. I quietly sat with her, asked if she was okay, and called her mother to pick her up. When she arrived, we all agreed that proper disposal was a *very* important topic, and after they left, I fished the offending wad of cotton out of the bowl and my husband out of the garage.

—Catherine Conant, Middletown, CT

Catherine Conant is a professional storyteller who has been performing, teaching, and coaching for more than fifteen years. Growing up in New Jersey, she called her period "Aunt Tillie from Red Bank."

Mattress Pad, 1990

My first encounter with a maxi pad happened when I was six. My mother was hosting a small dinner party, and I was around the house, finding my own entertainment. After I was finished with my coloring book, I started playing with a small doll. That became boring pretty quickly. I decided to go into my mom's room and look through her closet and chest of drawers—one of my favorite activities. This time, instead of finding shoes and necklaces, I came upon a small stack of pads. At that time, we were living in Russia, and sanitary pads were rarely sold in packaging. I did not know what they were back then; all I knew was that they were the same size as my doll. This led me to the most rational conclusion a six-year-old could come to: my mother had bought me doll mattresses and was waiting to give them to me as a present. Obviously! I took one out and proceeded to carry it, along with my doll, into the dining room. As the adults were sitting at the table talking to each other, I came up and sat on the adjacent couch. With tender love and care, I proceeded to meticulously arrange the maxi pad and put my doll to sleep on it. Once I was happy with my arrangement, I decided to show everyone my motherly abilities. I proudly placed my arrangement on the table. As soon as I did that, the adult chatter died down and was replaced by laughter. Red-faced, my mother whisked me away into the next room and gave me a crash course on menstruation.

I got my period when I was thirteen. I was playing outside with a few friends and ran inside to pee. As I looked down on my underwear, I noticed a large, reddish brown stain. I called for my mom and grandma, who came running over. I felt like I wasn't a kid anymore, that this was the beginning of the end. My body was starting to change, and this was the activation of my death sentence. It was all downhill from there. My mom gave me some pads, but this time I knew they weren't doll mattresses. Neither my mom nor my grandma made a big deal of it; they were very nonchalant. In a way, I wanted them to make it a big deal and I was a bit upset that they didn't. My grandmother said that I should not go swimming while I had my period. She still continues to tell me that over the phone, even though she knows I only wear tampons.

—Yulia, New York

Yulia is a founder and an editor of a postfeminist arts and literary magazine.

No Gushing for Me, Please, 1979

Periods, I knew from rumor, began with massive, embarrassing gushes of blood. Why would anyone look forward to that? I was thirteen and about to go to high school, and although some girls my age already used deodorant, shaved, and wore bras, I was, according to my mother, too young for all that nonsense. That was fine with me. Being a girl was fun. Besides, I was about to go to Kenya for the summer with my best friend and her parents. They were archaeologists and whenever she came home from a dig, she had platinum hair and skin as bronzed as a white girl's can be. Secretly, I hoped to transform myself from wallflower to supermodel before high school began.

The trip was great. We stayed on the island of Lamu. We bought kikois and wore them tied, local-girl style, around our necks; we sunbathed every day with lemon juice in our hair; and one day, coming home from the beach, I almost got arrested by a policeman who considered my bikini indecent. He said I was too much of a woman to expose all that skin. I was thrilled.

Back home, however, the mirror showed me the same mousy child. I was trying on my new Catholic-schoolgirl uniform, horrified that without an undershirt my nipples showed through the polyester blouse, when my mother came to me from the laundry room holding out a pair of my underwear. There in the crotch were those mysterious brown spots that had refused to come clean when I'd washed them by hand back in Lamu. She asked if I had gotten my period in Africa. Of course, I denied it. How could I have had a period without knowing it? She asked what the spots were then.

For a second, she had me. But then I saw my out. "Those are shit spots!" I said, as if shitting in one's pants was less embarrassing than having had a period without knowing it. With her silence, I felt I had won.

As it turned out, she was right about the spots; slowly, slowly over the next several years, the spotting grew heavier until I knew that this was my own version of menstruation. Still, the victory was mine. I was able to become a woman on my own terms without any gushing about it.

—Monica Wesolowska, Berkeley, CA

Monica is a fiction writer (although the above is entirely true).

The Slap, 1972

Our home had burned down a few days earlier in an electrical fire. As a result, I was living in a neighbor's house with my mom, while my brother and dad were living in another friend's house. I was feeling disoriented and worried because I didn't know the neighbors very well. What's more, my dog, who had been caught in the fire, was suffering from severe burns and smoke inhalation (she died a few months later).

I went to the bathroom at school and saw a brownish stain on my underwear.

I thought I must be ill with some sort of stomach virus but was confused because I felt just fine. I called my mother and told her what I had found. She sounded very excited, congratulated me on getting my period, and told me to wait in the bathroom because she would be there in a few minutes. When she arrived, she slapped me across the face and then hugged me. Stunned and even more confused, I asked her what I had done wrong. She began to laugh and told me that girls who get their first period are slapped and hugged to feel the pain and joy of womanhood. I decided that if I ever had a daughter, I would find a better way to mark the occasion.

—Ilene Lainer, New York, NY

Ilene is the founder and executive director of the New York Center for Autism. She and husband Steven have two sons, Max and Ari.

Editor's Note: It is an old custom to slap a young woman's face at the time of her first period. There are various explanations. One view is that it is intended to shock you out of childhood. Another explanation is that it is done to ward off the evil eye. Most women seem to have little idea of the origins of this ritual.

Rescued by a Refugee, 1941

In the fall of 1941, a month shy of fourteen, I went into the girls' room in my Bronx high school. In that cubicle, I began my first period.

I knew that it would happen to me one day. I can't honestly say how, because when I saw ads in my mother's *Ladies' Home Journal* for Modess or Kotex, their euphemisms—cloud-light and soft—were puzzling. I asked my mother and, evading my question, she left me in the land of mystery.

The only other girl in that bathroom was a French refugee, Odette. (Remember, it was World War II.)

I paid my nickel into the wall-hung machine, bought a sanitary napkin, and stood there, wondering how to attach it. Odette came to my rescue, showing me how to use the tiny safety pins enclosed.

When I walked home that afternoon, my mother met me halfway to inform me that I had my period.

"How do you know?" I wondered.

"Your pajamas," she replied, moving forward to give me a hug. And then she told me that the old-world custom was to slap a girl the first time, but that she was too modern to do such a primitive thing.

—Pearl Stein Selinsky, Sacramento, CA

Pearl is a retired schoolteacher and published writer who has two grown children and four grandsons.

The Wrath of the Gods, 1970

She walked to the back
of the hot bus, queasy from the smell
of gasoline, past the place where boys congregated,
checking out each girl that dared to pass
the unspoken initiation
to the tiny bathroom
suffocating as a confessional
to discover for the first time its dark stain.
After the raucous pounding (the boys beating on the door)
quieted, she emerged into the dim light
but nothing had changed.
No boy later that night slipped into the empty seat
to whisper in her ear.
No girls flocked around her to share
in the newfound glory.
If there were gods, they were sent here
for one purpose, to decree that out of abundance
was pain, and from suffering
perhaps one day a child.
At the top of the monument
that brought them on the journey
early that day, tired after their triumph
(eight hundred and ninety-seven stone steps!)
she knew she was at the edge
of something grand and momentous
where she could see the glimmer—
the Lincoln and Thomas Jefferson memorials

and our nation's Capitol, the dotted figures
of lovers strolling in the park,
the cherry trees in blossom!
of what lay beyond
the guarded, serpentine walls
of her suburban community
where she might one day
forge her independence.
On the mount she could feel the press
of sun anointing her face, the air
like joy, building inside her;
the presence of our founding fathers
no longer imposed their dense weight.
But it wasn't until her mother picked her up
at the high school in the twilight
after the journey
that she knew no one
(perhaps not even the gods)
was watching.
The stars trembled.
The restless moths went at the streetlamp.
In the yard crickets screeched.
Twigs snapped.
The red, poisonous berries
from the tree shading her driveway
shed on the windshield of their car.

—Jill Bialosky, Cleveland, OH

Jill Bialosky is a poet, a writer, and an editor. Her work has appeared in the New Yorker, *the* Paris Review, *and* O *magazine.*

Locked in a Room with Dosai, 1962

Till I was ten or eleven, every time I visited the Bangalore house, I would notice something strange. Some female family member would disappear mysteriously and appear later, maybe during the afternoon nap period, and sit apart from the rest of the family. We younger folk were warned not to touch her and were told it was a religious thing. After I started menstruating, I realized, "Aha, so that's what it was all about!" My older cousins and aunts now could not tease me or send me away during gossip sessions; I would be part of this elite female crew as well.

But I hated that all the male cousins knew what was happening and showed knowing smirks. *Paati* was very traditional, so she expected all of us to observe this ritual without fail. Why did this monthly cycle have to be broadcast? Fortunately, we stayed only for a month, so this embarrassment happened only once during the summer stay, though I did feel sorry for my cousins, who lived there.

Once you got your period, you could not enter the main part of the house. You were supposed to go to the back door and wait for someone to realize you were missing, and then notice you standing there. I had watched the different tactics aunts and cousins would employ to accomplish this. Once they realized that they were *It*, they would whisper to someone who was *Not It* and rush to the back door. Or they would tap on a nearby window to draw attention. Meanwhile, the annex room would be kept ready for this person.

Now the next step involved getting to the annex room through the backyard and the back garden. This little room was near the front of the house, with its own door.

The back garden was a piece of land with red earth and black, fuzzy caterpillars that terrified me. Gingerly, I would venture my way, closing my eyes, taking gentle steps to land in the annex room. I was an adult now. No, no, I could not be afraid of silly caterpillars. *Amma* would give me an encouraging smile, and I would look very composed and go quietly into that room.

The annex room was actually a pleasant, light room with lots of books and a nice bed. The room had two windows; one was hard to open, but the other, made up of four panel windows, two in the bottom and two at the top, could be opened to reveal bars. This window faced the street. I had seen my cousins when they were cloistered, carrying on chats with their friends standing on the street. I was the youngest initiate in this room, so my friends were the books.

When I needed to go to the bathroom, I had to do it all in reverse. I had to open the side door and walk back through the caterpillar-infested back garden to the bathroom. Some aunts yelled out, "I am coming!" to warn others, almost sounding like, "Caution! Menstruating woman on the loose!"

I would step out of the room, survey the area, and go through the war zone, looking and hoping that no child would come rushing out to touch me.

The male members found it amusing and aggravating, because if the isolated person happened to be their sister or mother, they could not sit and have a casual chat with her. Usually *It* would come out of the back room, and with help from the rest of the family, arrive safely in the big main room. There she could sit in a corner during the afternoons to chat and join in the fun and laughter, but no private conversations were possible. If you happened to be *It's* little child, your life turned upside down for the next four days. These little ones had no idea what was happening, so they would weep and wail for their mothers and go rushing to them, and no amount of *No, no, no!* could stop them. There were compromises, however. These children were allowed to run around naked since, if they were clothed, they had to be bathed immediately when they touched their mothers.

Oh, yes, food for *It* was also a complicated affair. Someone would serve *It* the food only after everyone had eaten. Also, *It* would be told to keep her plate and cups and wash them and keep them in her room.

The whole thing was complicated and stressful even to think about, but I felt I just had to do it; no questioning was allowed. This isolation and extra planning and work was also irksome, but all of us aunts and cousins meekly followed the four-day penance, since on release day we were rewarded with a special treat—*masala dosai*.

Now *dosai* is a very common food made of fermented lentil and rice batter and eaten in most South Indian homes. It looks like a crepe, only it is usually golden brown and crisp, eaten with butter and coconut chutney or a stewlike soup made with onions.

Paati would make this at home sometimes. She would

wait for her black flat griddle to get hot on her wood-burning stove, then she would expertly sweep the creamy white rice-lentil batter and spread it out thin and round on the griddle. When the *dosai* was done, she would add butter (freshly churned at home) and her special chutney so it was well covered. Then she put two spoonfuls of her potato-onion-*masala* mixture on one half of the *dosai* and expertly and effortlessly folded the other half over it. She would then add a little more butter and serve the folded *dosai*, hot and crisp, to a family member.

This whole process was tedious for one person to accomplish. And somehow, the special blend of chutneys and the crisp texture of the *dosai* was an altogether unique and delicious experience in Bangalore restaurants. The modest, triangularly shaped *dosai* with all the fillings inside was served with two kinds of chutney on the side as well!

Thatha would go to the local restaurant and return with the *dosai* wrapped in banana leaves. The warm smell of the chutneys and the melted butter would waft into the house as he walked in with a smile. I still remember this delectable dish on my release day, a "welcome back to the world" gift that meant all would be well for the next twenty-four days.

—Shobha Sharma, Chennai, India

Shobha Sharma came to the United States from India in 1976, planning to pursue a career in chemistry. After a few years, she realized that she would rather be a writer and open a feminist bookstore. Yippee! She recently finished a novel about the women of India.

Simple as Salt, 1967 and 2008

What I'd like to share is the huge difference between my getting my first period and my daughter getting her first period. I was playing baseball in the streets at my grandmother's when I felt a twisting pain in my belly and was shocked to find rusty stains in my underwear. Family was visiting that day—perhaps a dozen relatives. My grandmother went outside and made a general announcement: "Jacquelyn became a woman today! She got the curse!" I spent the day cowering in a dark bedroom, not only ashamed in front of my friends but certain I would never be able to face anyone again, particularly one leering old uncle, with anything but a face red as a swollen plum. Months before my own daughter's twelfth birthday, I built a "period" box from a Sephora container with a magnetized lid. In it were pads of various sizes, tampons, the very slimmest Q&A book I could find, and a bottle of Tylenol. When she came to me one winter night to report her first period, we spent an hour cuddling in my bed, and I told her, "This means your body is getting ready to be a woman, not that you are a woman. When you become a woman is up to you. For now, you can be a happy sixth-grade girl and still love sports and have boys who are friends and wear your ratty jeans and your Toledo Mud Hens T-shirt."

"That's a relief," Francie said. "I don't have to grow up?"

"Not until the minute you're ready."

"Can I still play sports when I have . . . my period?"

"Best thing for it," I told her. "That way you'll never

have the kind of crippling cramps girls used to get back in the day. You can do anything when you have your period that you can when you don't."

At her request, I taught her how to use a tampon for swim-team days. And so the dreaded, the hyperbolic, the sinister, the overblown drama that attended my own biological coming-of-age was folded into my daughter's life as neatly as getting a sports bra—a kind of annoying but ultimately important part of being female.

And for her sweet sake, I thanked God that—as I had for her much-older brothers when they first lost their virginity—I was as practical about sex as about salt, feeling, as I always had, that the right amount of it makes life so much better it's astonishing, and that too much of it can ruin a personality as easily as it can ruin a piecrust.

When I am tempted to think—as I often am—that I'm so tired of how much has "almost changed," I think of this comfort of communication—how awful it was for me and how much worse it was for my friends in the 1960s and 1970s, some of whom got nothing except a box of pads and a terse note about unplanned pregnancy shoved into their closets the summer before seventh grade. One friend's mom had six daughters and never once discussed ovulation, menstruation, or contraception with any of them.

Much has changed, and much of it for the better.

—Jacquelyn Mitchard, Madison, WI

Jacquelyn Mitchard is the best-selling author of seven books for teens and eight adult novels. Her novel The Deep End of the

Ocean was the first book to be chosen by Oprah's Book Club and was named by USA Today *as one of the ten most influential books of the past twenty-five years. She has seven children, each of whom she talks to every day. She is very organized.*

Editor's Note: Is Jacquelyn Mitchard the chillest mom ever, or what?

Señorita, 1980

My story begins about five years before I got my actual period. We had moved from Puerto Rico to Trinidad and were living in an apartment until we could find a house to live in. I remember one day picking up a piece of red candy from a bowl, popping it into my mouth, and sucking on it for a while. I didn't like it, and since I was in the bathroom at the time, I simply threw the candy into the commode and flushed. Several hours later, my mother yelled for all of us girls (I am the youngest of four siblings; three of us are female) to come to the bathroom immediately. She started grilling us about who had used the bathroom last, whether any of us were sick or bleeding, and whether any of us had gotten our period. We all denied it and asked her why. She finally showed us the water in the bowl; it was bright red. I then realized that the culprit was the candy and told her. The relief on her face was immediately apparent, and we all started laughing. She used the opportunity to explain to us yet again about periods. We already knew; having seen the giant boxes of sanitary napkins prominently displayed in her bathroom when she was menstruating, each of us had at some point inquired about them and been told.

In Latino culture, getting your period is a significant event, a time when you become a señorita. When my other two sisters got their periods, my mother announced it to the family at the dinner table with great pride. That was a bit much for me. I was fourteen when mine finally arrived. It was in the morning, and I was on my way to school. I simply changed my underwear, put on a sanitary napkin, and went to school. My mother found out eventually when she asked me about it. She was clearly hurt that I had not voluntarily shared this intimacy with her.

It would be a full year before she would finally agree to buy us tampons. Preserving your virginity until marriage in the Latino culture was sacrosanct, and my mother was a great believer. Unfortunately, that also meant not being able to wear tampons until you were married, lest it tamper with your hymen. The three of us girls rebelled at the dinner table one day. We made a case by pointing out to her that most of our girlfriends at school wore tampons and that it impeded our ability to play sports (especially swimming). When my father spoke up in our support, she relented. Relief! For me, being able to wear tampons was a more momentous occasion than getting my period.

—Kica Matos, New Haven, CT

Kica is a lawyer who defended death-row inmates and now runs the Community Services Agency for the City of New Haven.

Can I Sit on His Lap? 1916

I was eleven years old. I had a friend where I lived, and her parents had a store. She and I were very good friends, but it was very, very long ago, and I have forgotten her name. I was riding her tricycle once when I felt something sticky between my legs.

I went up to my mother, which was the usual thing when I didn't understand something. I didn't know what it was. I had no idea that it was blood. I'd never heard about it in my life, because at the time they never told children about these things.

Well, she took a look, and she said, "Ooohh, *shoin* [Yiddish for *already*]?" She didn't expect me to have this. Then she washed me and explained what it was. She took a rag, that handy rag, and pinned it to what I was wearing, and at that moment I felt as if *something has happened in my life . . .* and isn't it wonderful?

Later that day, my father took me for a walk to the nearby East River. As we sat on a bulkhead where the ships came in, I said to him, "You know what I'm going to get every month?" I saw him wince, and he said, hesitating and very embarrassed, "Uh, yeah, yeah." And I said, "A girl told me that I mustn't sit on any man's lap or on any boy's lap, because it's very dangerous when you get that." My friend had said, "Keep away from men or boys until you get older." So I turned to him and asked, "Do I have to keep away from men and boys?" Again, he was very uncomfortable and, after thinking for a moment, said, "Well, I don't know. Maybe it's better that you don't."

—Henrietta Wittenberg, Now York, NY

Henrietta lived to the age of 101. She loved music and singing. Born in New York City, she spent the last years of her life at Tower One in New Haven, where she was known as "the dancing lady."

Barbies and Biology, 1996

On January 6, 1996, I experienced my initiation into the world of women. I was to turn twelve in less than two months, and my life seemed the most ordinary kind of life anybody could be living. One Saturday evening, I noticed a largish red spot on my underwear, and it felt almost expected. I went to the living room and whispered to my mother that she needed to come to the bathroom. I showed her the red spot, refraining from any words or explanations. She reminded me that I knew where we kept the pads, and she helped me get set up. Back then, my mother used the cushion-sized maxi pads and, strangely enough, the extra thickness made me feel more secure.

Though the night of my first period was anything but traumatic, school was different. I had a close circle of friends who shared every secret. Nobody among my friends had mentioned anything about bleeding, and I was convinced that something was wrong with me if I had developed quicker than they had. I felt very awkward keeping this personal piece of information to myself, but I was afraid of being ostracized for being abnormal. This struggle went on for a whole day of school. The strong urge to disclose my secret to my best friend won over my fear, and I decided to tell her on Tuesday. I initiated the conversation, stating that I had a secret. She surprised me by saying that she, too, had a secret. After going through quite a few disclaimers, we found out that we were both talking about the same secret, two days apart. Getting that off our chests, we shared our experiences and had a new desire to find out if others in our classroom had such a secret. Before long, we found out that many of our female classmates were going through the same thing and had not been able to tell anyone else.

The next few weeks, we spent our days talking about our menstruation with the code name "Barbie." We could talk about getting our Barbies out loud without the boys' having the slightest clue. Initially, some boys guessed that our whispering in small circles had to be about sexuality, since that was all there was to be talked about. Later, they were convinced that, with such enthusiasm, we must have been talking about blonde skinny dolls.

It was not until a year later that we found out more about the biology of menstruation. All the middle-school girls were taken out of class one day for what we later found out was an information session sponsored by Orkid (the Always brand in Turkey). It was informational but abstract. I still wondered for many years afterward what caused the bleeding. I had heard that the canal to one's uterus was closed by a very important piece of membrane, the hymen. In my logic, since everything else is kept inside, then it must be the hymen that bleeds each month. It was not till senior year of high school that I found out the hymen had openings that let the blood through. Afterward, ashamed of my own ignorance, I began sharing all the information I had regarding female anatomy among my friends. The truth is, so many of us go through life hoping that someone else knows how everything functions inside our own cavities.

—Aysegul Altintas, Istanbul, Turkey

Aysegul is a native of Turkey. She studied molecular, cellular, and developmental biology at Yale and is pursuing a Ph.D. at Sabanci University.

An excerpt from "Letters"

Just married, one day pregnant, you blushed
so pink Niagara's fabled sunset paled.
"Papa will kill me when he hears," you quailed
but the first grandchild, a boy, softened the blow.
You told me how your mother had slapped your face

the day your first blood caked along your thighs,
then sent you to your sister for advice.
Luckier, I was given *Marjorie May's
Twelfth Birthday*, a vague tract printed by Kotex,
so vague it led me to believe you bled
that one year only, and chastely left unsaid
the simple diagrammatics about sex.
When was it that I buried Muzz, began
to call you by the name that blazoned Woman?

—Maxine Kumin, New Hampshire

100

Maxine Kumin has been both the U.S. and the New Hampshire Poet Laureate.

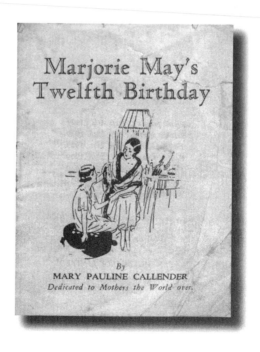

My Support System Was a Box, 1977

My mother was forty-one when she had me and was menopausal by the time I was five. Growing up, I remember that there were no feminine hygiene products around at all. I had three older brothers, and I don't ever remember having a conversation at home about bodies, sex, or anything related to periods. I knew about periods from friends, not from home.

One day when I was in seventh grade, a package arrived in the mail. It came from Kotex and was addressed to my mom. I thought this was odd, since she would not need to be ordering supplies. When my mom wasn't around, I snooped around to track it down and discovered that it was a sampler kit of all sorts of Kotex products, booklets (one that I remember was titled something like "How to Discuss This with Your Daughter"), belts, and other antiquated items.

The day that I got my period, my mom was away. I called her to ask what I should do, and she said, "Well, there is this box. . . ."

Periods were never discussed before and have never been discussed since. My entire support system was a box.

—Bonnie Garmisa, Guilford, CT

A native of Chicago, Bonnie has lived for fourteen years in Guilford with husband Tom; children Clara, Ellie, and Simon; and dog Hugo.

Jaws, 2004

That day, it wasn't dark or stormy. The calm turquoise ocean glowed, and the warm dust of the sun painted the rickety fishing boat gold and toasted my poor excuse for breasts. I was on that boat, absorbed in some childish daydream, ignoring the captain's lectures about straying too far from the group once we were out, safety, blah, blah, and blah. I flopped my rubber flippers with the rhythm of the salty waves. The farther the little ship huffed and puffed away from the white shore, the more impatient I grew, the more I ached to submerge myself in the mysterious Caribbean Sea and pretend I was a fish or something.

Finally, we slowed, and a guy threw the anchor overboard into the beautiful, sparkly depths. More dumb lectures from the captain that I didn't listen to. My snorkel was strapped so tightly to my face that my eyeballs felt like popping out, and my adult-sized lifejacket hung loose on my twelve-year-old frame. I thought I was hot stuff as I waddled to the back of the boat and was second only to the anchor to toss myself into the water. My abdomen cramped and burned with joy as I gazed longingly into the magical empire that was this coral reef. Little eels wove around anemones exploding with color. Hypnotized, I found myself paddling along with a school of huge yellow tuna fish until I realized that I had ventured into darker and less lively waters. But alas, I was not afraid. I was an explorer, goddamn it!

A leak can attract unwanted attention

TAMPAX
PEARL
PLASTIC

REGULAR

fresh scent

Helps prevent leaks

And I explored and explored, and found nothing except that I was swimming farther from the boat and farther from the ocean floor. I also found that my whole stomach was bubbling painfully, and as I looked down, there was a deep red cloud swirling with the murky blue water between my legs. In that moment, I lifted my head and looked up at the sky through my foggy goggles. In that moment, far from my family, the boat, the captain, the sea anemones, I became a woman. A bit blood-soaked, but a woman! In the moment following that moment, I spotted a large gray fin coming toward me,

which turned out to be a

dolphin!

—Lily Gottchalk, Wallingford, CT

Lily is a quirky being who often writes sea-themed poems. (She has a particular affinity for narwhals.) If she could have relived her first period, she would have laughed more.

Dying in the Land of Dionysus, 1972

There seems to be a common thread that girls get their first periods when away from their mothers. I was ten years old and traveling in Greece with my family the summer between fourth and fifth grades. One of my classmates, Maria, was Greek and spent each summer in Athens. We were thrilled, as kids are, at the thought of seeing each other under unusual circumstances.

I am the child of Chinese immigrants who placed the ultimate value on a first-class education but for whom imparting firsthand knowledge was, and remains, difficult. My mother and I are very close, but we did not have the milestone discussions about menstruation, boyfriends, or sex. I remember vividly when the topic of menstruation was introduced in fourth-grade health education class. I embarrassed myself by raising my hand and asking, "How long does the period last?" The teacher somewhat impatiently replied that this had already been covered and that a period could last for five to eight days. But I was wondering if the bleeding only occurred between certain hours each day.

That summer, just after we had arrived in Athens, Maria and her mother came to the hotel to take me to their summer home on the beach. I had never been on a motorboat before and could hardly contain my excitement. When getting into my new bathing suit (a blue one-piece with a little skirt), I noticed that I had stained my underwear. Not for a moment did I connect the blood with the classroom lesson on menstruation. Instead I chose to ignore it, hoping it would simply stop. So there I was on a boat in my new blue bathing suit, bleeding. I continued to bleed over the next two days while with my friend's family. I didn't mention it to anyone, because beyond the embarrassment was the fear that I was dying.

My friend's mother eventually caught on and took me back to the hotel to my mother. In her total awareness of me and my needs, my mother had planned for this possibility and packed a supply of small sanitary napkins and a belt. I could tell from her manner that I wasn't sick. At last I put two and two together and figured out that I was having my first period. You might wonder why it took me that long to come to this conclusion, but at ten, I was young and unprepared. Of course, I vowed that it would not happen that way with my own daughters, but as life turned out, I have three sons. I suspect that even if I'd had a daughter, some unplanned circumstance would have arisen, because that just seems to be the way of first periods.

—Mary Hu, New Haven, CT

Mary is director of strategic development and marketing at the Yale Medical Group. She is an avid knitter and the mother of three sons.

Step Toward Womanhood, but with Stepmom, 1983

By the time I was eleven, I'd been expecting my period for two years. My mother's had come at age nine and, in what seemed to me the physical embodiment of their philosophical differences, my stepmother's had arrived at age eighteen. I planned to get mine early, too, as a way of aligning myself with my mother. I assumed my body would comply.

No such luck. In fact, I was with my stepmother, and nearly every other member of my father's extended family, when my period finally showed up—a splotch of brownish red in the crotch of the brand-new OP bathing suit that my stepmother had just purchased for me. New clothes were a rare treat when I was growing up—we wore Salvation

Army and hand-me-downs almost exclusively. I was sporting this miraculous vestment at my cousin's bar mitzvah afterparty on Long Island, with kids whose hard accents and knowing suburban ways seemed so foreign to a college-town kid like me. I looked terrible in my swimsuit. My new breasts poked sadly from behind the pastel rainbows, and hair peeked from beneath the fabric at my leg creases. One boy called me Elephant Girl. Apparently he liked me.

In the bathroom, I discovered the marring of my beautiful-but-not-on-me suit. It was so anticlimactic. Here I'd been hungering for my period for two years, beginning to feel something was wrong with me, lying about it on occasion to girls whose bodies were faster to arrive at puberty. And there it was: nothing more than a stain on my fancy suit. The main feeling, besides the dull ache in my lower back, which would worsen as the years and periods went on, was guilt: my reproductive system had betrayed my mother, forcing me to go to my stepmother with the news, seek her advice, her solace.

I couldn't do it. With "Hava Nagila" blaring in the background, I approached my aunt and stepmother and asked casually if either had a tampon, a word I'd learned in anticipation of this day. I pretended I was an old hat at handling periods; pretended, as I'd sometimes done with my friends, that I'd endured many periods before. I don't think they bought it. They looked at one another knowingly, then leaned down and asked, "How about a pad?" But they asked me no more questions.

When my period came again, I was back at my mother's house, wearing my same old vintage clothes. I hadn't told her about my bar mitzvah period, and I could have pretended now that this was my first, giving her the great satisfaction of sharing that monumental occasion with me. I felt that battle inside me, torn between the miserable shyness I shared with her about the Big Issues—talks about the birds and the bees or drugs were mumbled and perfunctory—and the desire to please her, a single mother with a low-paying job and an ex who rarely paid child support.

The shyness won. I casually asked her the same question I'd uttered the month before—Do you have a tampon? She, too, looked at me tenderly, if perhaps a little hurt that I hadn't included her more. And she asked, "How about a pad?"

—Lisa Selin Davis, Brooklyn, NY

Lisa is the author of a novel, Belly, *and a freelance journalist. She writes about real estate, architecture, and the environment for the* New York Times, New York *magazine,* Grist *magazine,* Brownstoner.com, *and other publications.*

Yodelay Uh-Oh, 1982

Forgive me, but I was wearing overalls—the OshKosh B'Gosh train-conductor kind—and a pink bandanna on my head. I had turned twelve that summer, but I still had no inkling of a chest, and my mother still braided my long blonde hair into braids. I was walking our two goats on dog leashes in the grassy yard of my family's summer place in eastern Canada—a veritable Heidi. The air smelled like fresh-cut hay. I could see my mother through the large kitchen window, making herself a salad from *The Beverly Hills Diet*. She was down to 102 pounds. I was singing to myself. "Karma Chameleon." "With a Rebel Yell." I was neither a chameleon nor a rebel . . . yet. But I had kissed boys. I had stolen a Popsicle. I owned a pair of tight green velvet Gloria Vanderbilt jeans and a fake fur jacket. I'd even gotten drunk once. I had potential.

The goats were tugging me toward the lilac bush, which was strictly off-limits, when I felt it, hot and sticky, in my underwear. I'd read *Are You There God? It's Me, Margaret*. I'd even tried on one of those gigantic maxi pads they supply on airplanes. I'd questioned the older girls at school. I knew what this was. I even knew where my mother kept her tampons. I dashed into the house.

Our sex-ed teacher, who happened to be my brother's psychiatrist's wife, had demonstrated how a tampon works by pushing it out of the applicator into a bottle of water. The instructions on the side of the box of o.b.'s looked complicated and required way too much finger action. Where was the applicator?

"Mummy?" I yelled, my face red with embarrassment. I couldn't remember the last time I'd called her into the bathroom. Recently I'd spent a lot of time trying to shut her *out*.

"Oh!" she gasped when I showed her my lightly blood-smirched underpants. "Well, I'll be damned. You do know what that is, don't you?"

I rolled my eyes. She picked up the box of o.b.'s.

"Those won't work," I interjected.

"Well," she said brightly. "I guess we'll have to go shopping!" She rummaged around below the sink and found an almost-empty box of panty liners. Then she fetched me a pair of clean underwear and went to tell my father.

When I sat down to dinner, my father expressed his annoyance that we would be gone for most of the day tomorrow. He'd wanted to take out our speedboat and have a picnic. But the nearest stores were more than an hour away, and if we were going to go, we might as well make a day of it, buying groceries at the SaveEasy and clothes at Zellers, the only clothing store in town.

"Can't you just stuff a rag or an old towel up there?" my father asked.

Needless to say, we went shopping.

—Cecily von Ziegesar, Brooklyn, NY

Cecily von Ziegesar is the author of The It Girl *and* Gossip Girls *series, the latter of which has been turned into a highly addictive TV show. Cecily has two children and a balding cat named Pony Boy.*

The White Dress, 1971

I was very late starting my period—fifteen or sixteen—and was beginning to worry, as all my friends had already gone through several years of having their periods. I once had very light spotting and thought, "Okay, this is it." But then nothing came for months. Mom called the doctor and he said that it would come when it was time. (No one even thought about my being sexually active—I wasn't, but *no one* even thought it!!!)

The summer between my junior and senior years in high school, I went to Europe to study French. It was my first time flying. I had to fly from Cleveland to New York and then to Rome. We were barely in the air when I felt something gush. And I do mean gush! I was so embarrassed. I was wearing a white sundress and fortunately had a sweater with me. I waited till everyone got off the plane in New York and then I tied the sweater around me and escaped. There was blood on the seat and everything, but I didn't say a word because I was too embarrassed. My mother had made me pack a change of clothes in my carry-on and some pads (since the ones in Europe at that time were awful. "Just in case," she said). Thank heavens she did. I went into the bathroom and changed, but I couldn't do anything about the dress. When I finally got to Rome—sixteen hours later—I tried to wash it in the sink, but no luck, so I wadded it up in a corner of my suitcase.

After Rome and Paris, I was to live with a French family for a month. I came home after my first day of classes and found that all my clothes had been washed. The dress was immaculate! I still don't know how my host mom did it. And I was *way* too embarrassed to say anything except thank you for doing my laundry.

—Kathi Kovacic, Cleveland, OH

Kathi Kovacic is a retired librarian.

Up at the Chalkboard, 1979

I was thirteen years old, tall, and lanky. I had just sat for my common entrance examination to high school. The results were not yet in, and the full school session was not yet out, so the teachers organized classes preparing us for high school. The boys in my class described me as arrogant and proud and said that I loved to rub shoulders with them. This was because I was always the top-ranked or second-highest-ranking student, and that angered them. I was aware of my academic superiority over them, so I also threw my weight about a little, but my first period was to humble me.

In my well-ironed purple school uniform, the class teacher had asked me to go up to the chalkboard to solve a math problem. Completely oblivious of the big, dark brown patch on the back of my dress, I walked defiantly, as usual, to go and display my mathematical acumen. I heard giggles, which grew louder, and then thunderous laughter. I turned around, and someone pointed to the back of my dress. I turned, and there it was.

I thought I was sick and dying. I rushed to the bathroom and grew even more horrified. That was my first time ever to know that something like this existed and was part of womanhood. Nobody had ever told me anything about it. I just burst out crying. I was scared. I wrapped a cardigan around my waist and went home crying, told my mother, and guess what? She referred me to my big sister, who did not explain what was going on but gave me a huge pad. She did tell me, though, that I should expect this experience every month. She also warned me that now that I'd had my period, a sexual relationship would make me pregnant!

And guess what else? The boys in my class, and the girls who had not experienced it yet, taunted me badly in the days that followed. Bottom line? I was a bad girl to have blood ooze out of my private parts!

—Emilia Arthur, Accra, Ghana

In 2004, Emilia Arthur ran for Parliament in Ghana. She is currently director of an NGO called Integrated Action for Development Initiative, which works to strengthen local development.

If Men Could Menstruate

A white minority of the world has spent centuries conning us into thinking that a white skin makes people superior—even though the only thing it really does is make you more subject to ultraviolet rays and to wrinkles. Male human beings have built whole cultures around the idea that penis envy is "natural" to women—though having such an unprotected organ might be said to make men vulnerable, and the power to give birth makes womb envy at least as logical.

In short, the characteristics of the powerful, whatever they may be, are thought to be better than the characteristics of the powerless—and logic has nothing to do with it.

What would happen, for instance, if suddenly, magically, men could menstruate and women could not?

The answer is clear—menstruation would become an enviable, boast-worthy, masculine event:

Men would brag about how long and how much.

Boys would mark the onset of menses, that longed-for proof of manhood, with religious ritual and stag parties.

Congress would fund a National Institute of Dysmenorrhea to help stamp out monthly discomforts.

Sanitary supplies would be federally funded and free. (Of course, some men would still pay for the prestige of commercial brands such as Tiger Woods Tampons, Arnold Schwarzenegger Terminator Pads,

Michael Phelps Jock Shields—"For Those Light Bachelor Days." Indeed, Tampax could become the Official Tampon of the Men's Olympic Swim Team.

Military men, right-wing politicians, and religious fundamentalists would cite menstruation ("men-stru-ation") as proof that only men could serve in the army ("you have to give blood to take blood"), occupy political office ("can women be aggressive without that steadfast cycle governed by the planet Mars?"), be priests and ministers ("how could a woman give her blood for our sins?"), or rabbis ("without the monthly loss of impurities, women remain unclean").

Male radicals, left-wing politicians, mystics, however, would insist that women are equal, just different, and that any woman could enter their ranks if she were willing to self-inflict a major wound every month ("you MUST give blood for the revolution"), recognize the preeminence of menstrual issues, or subordinate her selfness to all men in their Cycle of Enlightenment. Street guys would brag ("I'm a three-pad man") or answer praise from a buddy ("Man, you lookin' good!") by giving fives and saying, "Yeah, man, I'm on the rag!" TV shows would treat the subject at length. (*The M Word* would break the taboo by dramatizing nothing else. *Law & Order* would have an endless source of DNA, *Mad Men* would satirize the old days before tampons, and all those modern HBO vampires—well, need I say more?) So would newspapers. (SHARK SCARE THREATENS MENSTRUATING MEN. JUDGE CITES MONTHLY

STRESS IN PARDONING RAPIST. LUNAR TERRORISM. HILLARY CLINTON: IS AMERICA READY FOR A BLOODLESS PRESIDENT?) And movies (*Blood Brothers*, starring George Clooney and Brad Pitt, and *Godfather III: Menopause*). Not to mention an Internet full of Moon chat rooms, cramp bloggers, and guys googling the rich and famous to find who's on the same schedule.

Men would convince women that intercourse was more pleasurable at "that time of the month." Lesbians would be said to fear blood and therefore life itself—though probably only because they needed a good menstruating man.

Of course, male intellectuals would offer the most moral and logical arguments. How could a woman master any discipline that demanded a sense of time, space, mathematics, or measurement, for instance, without that built-in gift for measuring the cycles of the moon and planets—and thus for measuring anything at all? In the rarefied fields of philosophy and religion, could women compensate for missing the rhythm of the universe? Or for their lack of symbolic death-and-resurrection every month?

Liberal males in every field would try to be kind: the fact that "these people" have no gift for measuring life or connecting to the universe, the liberals would explain, should be punishment enough.

And how would women be trained to react? One can imagine traditional women agreeing to all arguments with a staunch and smiling masochism. ("The

ERA would force housewives to wound themselves every month," Phyllis Schlafly. "Your husband's blood is as sacred as that of Jesus—and so sexy, too!" Sarah Palin.) Reformers and Queen Bees would try to imitate men and pretend to have a monthly cycle. All feminists would explain endlessly that men, too, needed to be liberated from the false idea of Martian aggressiveness, just as women needed to escape the bonds of menses envy. Radical feminists would add that the oppression of the nonmenstrual was the pattern for all other oppressions. ("Vampires were our first freedom fighters!") Cultural feminists would develop a bloodless imagery in art and literature. Socialist feminists would insist that only under capitalism would men be able to monopolize menstrual blood. . . .

In fact, if men could menstruate, the power justifications could probably go on forever.

If we let them.

—Gloria Steinem, New York, NY

Gloria is one of the twentieth century's most renowned feminists. She founded the National Women's Political Caucus and Choice USA, among other organizations. She is the author of Outrageous Acts and Everyday Rebellions.

Editor's Note: Ms. Steinem updated her essay for *My Little Red Book*. The essay originally appeared in *Ms.* magazine (1978), a publication she also founded. You can see the original version at www.mylittleredbook.net.

A Puddle, 1991

I get my period when I am in the seventh grade. In the morning it is one single red brown dot at the center of my panties. I am embarrassed. Annoyed. By the time I get to school, my period is heavy. I bleed through a pad in an hour. Inside my locker, I keep stacks of soft pink squares wrapped in plastic. I wedge them inside my purse one at a time when no one is looking. They make noise next to my Chapstick and house key.

In English, listening to the teacher diagram a sentence, I can feel it. The blood between my thighs runs and fills the pad, the wet stickiness warm and gushy. I sit very still, my thighs pressed together. I have twenty minutes before class lets out. There is no silent reading today, so I can't leave with a bathroom pass to change my pad. I stare at my notebook while wrapping my fingers around the edge of the plastic desk, trying to avoid any gum. I slide my fingers down onto the cool metal of the arm and focus on that instead of my rag. I can't possibly ask to be excused. All my pads are in my purse. Everyone will know when I stand up why I take my purse with me to the bathroom. She's so gross, they'll think. Yuck, look at her. It will be just like Carrie. Plug it up, they'll scream at me.

I shift in my seat and then I look, look in between my legs to see if any has gotten on the chair and it has. Blood is on the chair! I have tissue and when no one is looking, I slide it under my thighs. I will my period to stop. I squeeze my insides, but I feel the blood ooze and seep. I begin to chant: stop, stop, stop, stop. Closing my eyes, I imagine the little vessels closing up and shutting their mouths or that my body is like a faucet and all I have to do is shut it off. I do this in my head, turning harder and harder to off. But all I see is the blood squirting everywhere. Ten minutes left. Blood is on the tissue. Blood is wet against the upper thighs of my jeans. Wet. I take away bloody fingers. And then the bell rings and I slowly order my books on my desk. Take my time until the whole class leaves. And then I stand up and look at the blood on the plastic chair. I hurry up to the teacher's desk and tell her I left a puddle.

—Laura Madeline Wiseman, Arizona

Laura is a graduate student and a community activist.

Out of the Closet, 1968

A number of years back, I wrote a book about my life, including the story of what happened when I was a young girl, growing up. When this book was published, a great many of the people whose profession it is to read other people's books and say what they think about them, offered the opinion that I had committed a terrible offense in writing as I had. Of all the words in the English language, there was one, more than any other, that these critics and opinion-givers chose to apply to my writing and, more than that, to me as a human being, for having written as I had in my book—namely, for having told the truth. That word was "shameless." I gathered, from the rest of what these people wrote, that this was supposed to be a bad thing.

I was in my forties when I published this shameless book of mine, the story of my life. My three children were teenagers, my daughter right around the age I was when many of the experiences that formed some of the hardest parts of my story took place. I remember thinking how odd it was that I, of all people, would have been labeled a woman without shame—because more than most girls I knew, I grew up feeling so much of it. I knew from personal experience what it was like for a person to go through her days in fear that other people—even people she cared about and liked—might discover who she really was.

Looking back now on all the aspects of my life that used to make me ashamed, a curious thing strikes me: none of the things that caused me to feel this way—the fact that my father was an alcoholic, the fact that my mother was different from other people's mothers, the fact that I was still a virgin when so many of the girls around me were not—had anything to do with failures of character or what I might now regard as immoral behavior. I was embarrassed simply to be myself. And among the many things that caused shame in me, one of the worst was my period.

I knew it was coming. Every other girl in my class had

already gotten hers. In fact, before I started being ashamed of getting my period, I was ashamed of not getting my period. I was fourteen years old: two years had passed since the gym teacher first sat us down to show us the menstruation movie, and almost as long since my best friend, Becky, started carrying around sanitary napkins and wearing a bra. I, alone among the girls, still wore an undershirt that I tried to conceal by making large efforts to get to the locker room before anyone else so I could change in the bathroom stall. In fact, my breasts had begun to develop a little, but my mother didn't seem to have noticed, or to have done anything about it, and I was too ashamed—there was that word again—to ask her if we could buy me a bra. I was too ashamed to say the word "bra." Let alone "menstruation" or "period."

Then it happened. Blood in my underpants. By this time my older sister was gone from home, and my mother didn't get her period anymore, so there were no supplies in our house for taking care of things. And to get help I would have had to say what had happened. Unthinkable. Shame again.

I rode my bike into the town where we lived, and I walked into the store. But how was I to take the box down off the shelf, carry it to the front of the store, face the cashier to pay, and watch while she placed it in the bag? (I would have to choose a female cashier, at least. Having to reveal to a man or a boy this terrible, shameful need of mine would have been unbearable.)

My mission was hard enough. I tried to conceal or at least camouflage the nature of what I was up to by placing many other items in my basket along with the pads: a pencil, a tube of toothpaste, a notebook, bobby pins. Still, there was no hiding the blue box.

When I got home, I stuffed the pad in my underpants. But now there was a new problem: how to dispose of it when it was used up, soaked with my own shameful blood? If I put it in the wastebasket my mother would discover it. I could carry it down to the garage and place the used pad directly into our trash can, but how to get it through the rooms without being seen? How to explain the reason why, all of a sudden, I was making all these trips to the garage?

So I wrapped the used pad in toilet paper, placed it in a brown paper bag—the bag from the store where I'd bought the pads in the first place, probably—and stuck the whole thing in the back of my closet, and as I used more pads, I put them there. When my period was over, instead of disposing of this bag, I chose to leave it in the closet. And when my period came back, I added more used pads, always wrapped in toilet paper, to the ones that had been there before, taking pains not to look too deep in the bag.

Months passed like that. The bag had been large enough, and my periods were short enough in duration, that the same one bag continued to hold sanitary napkins from as much as a half-year's worth of periods. I still hadn't told my mother I menstruated. She didn't ask. The fact that she did not confirmed for me the belief that what went on in my body now was truly, deeply, horribly shameful.

Though it was not as shameful as what followed, the day

my mother discovered the bag of old used pads and confronted me with its contents. The blood was dried now. The pads were stiff with age. Bugs infested the pads now.

I considered not writing that last piece of the story, because telling you that part could make me ashamed, but then I remind myself to consider who was this girl who felt a need to hide her used, bloody sanitary napkins in her closet? Just a young, scared person so uncomfortable with her own self she had to conceal something as natural as what was going on inside her own body.

My mother wasn't angry. She wasn't a monster, or anything close. Looking back now on how poorly she handled the task of shepherding her younger daughter through puberty and the experience of first menstruation, I can only guess that shame of her own lay at the root of the problem. I didn't know this at the time, but years later—when we were finally able to talk about it—she told me that after my birth, when she was thirty-one, she didn't get her period again for twenty years, though strangely, it started up again after her marriage to my father was over. When she was finally happy.

So she found out about my period. But there remained a hundred other things—a thousand, a million—I could not have discussed with her, or anyone. Words I could not speak. Questions I couldn't ask anyone, so I lived with fear and uncertainty about their answers.

It didn't happen all at once, this transformation of mine from a girl too ashamed to speak the word "period" to one who could publish a book in which she spoke intimate truths about things that happened with a man, when she was young that should not have happened, about feeling so uncomfortable with her body that she almost stopped eating entirely, and how when she did eat, she stuck her finger down her throat, after, to get the calories out.

For me, I think, it was the experience of becoming a mother myself that made me know I must not allow my children to experience the kind of shame I grew up feeling. Maybe I went overboard in the opposite direction, but at our house we talked about things. If something made me uncomfortable, I didn't want to stick it in the back of the closet. I didn't want my sons and my daughter feeling as I had when I was young. And the only way I knew to teach them it was all right to talk about the difficult subjects was to do that myself.

So there you are. I am a shameless woman, according to my critics. And I am a shameless woman, to my family and friends. And the fact is, they are right about that. I will be ashamed if I hurt someone I love. I will be ashamed if I fail to be a good parent, a good person, a good citizen. I will not be ashamed that I bleed. Or—now, forty years later—that I seem to have stopped bleeding. It's just nature. It's just my body. It's just life. What in the world is so shameful about that?

—Joyce Maynard, Mill Valley, CA

In 1973, Joyce Maynard came to national attention with the publication of her New York Times *magazine cover story, "An*

Eighteen-Year-Old Looks Back on Life." Since then, she has written eleven books, including the memoir At Home in the World, *and the novel* To Die For. *She lives part-time at Lake Atitlan, Guatemala, where she runs the Lake Atitlan Writing Workshop, and in California, where she also teaches the art of making pie.*

Staining the Citroën, 1970

My parents and I lived in a small town on the Oregon coast, and on Sundays we would drive over the mountains to a Portland suburb, where we attended the Presbyterian church and visited my elderly grandmother.

After a midafternoon Sunday dinner at my grandmother's house, we got in our car and headed back over the mountains, normally about a two-hour drive. Our family car was a Citroën, imported from France and carefully maintained by my father. It had pale gray felt-upholstered seats, and the rule was that no eating or drinking was allowed inside the car at any time. When I visited the bathroom before leaving the house, I had discovered that I had gotten my first period, and being shy and embarrassed, decided not to tell anyone about it until I was safely home (where I knew the necessary supplies were stashed at the bottom of my chest of drawers). I tried to perch on the edge of the seat, as I was horrified that I might find a huge red spot when I got out of the car. Unfortunately, on that particular trip, our trusty family vehicle decided to break down about halfway home. There were no gas stations or any other signs of civilization anywhere close by, as we were near the summit of the mountain pass. My dad figured out that the problem had something to do with the radiator, so he hiked down to the creek to get enough water to get us home. This of course seemed to take *forever*, and I was starting to panic, as I had no idea how much blood was involved in one's first period.

We finally were able to get back on the road and were home by early evening. I was so relieved when I got out of the car and found no spots on the seat, nor on my Sunday clothes. I went straight to my bedroom and put on a pad that seemed to be about a foot long and a couple of inches thick— this was before the invention of adhesive strips on sanitary napkins, so it took some work to figure out the belt system— and finally got up the nerve to tell my mom what had happened. Fortunately, she didn't make too big a fuss, though as I recall, she did utter those famous words, "You are a woman now!"

—Catherine Johnson-Roehr, Bloomington, IN

Catherine grew up in Tillamook, Oregon, and now lives in Bloomington with her partner, Susan. She is the curator of art, artifacts, and photographs for the Kinsey Institute for Research in Sex, Gender, and Reproduction at Indiana University.

Cranberry Sauce, 1993

I t's tradition." It seemed that when my mother couldn't come up with a convincing, captivating reason behind something, it was quickly attributed to tradition. (Strangely enough, none of my relatives were familiar with our "traditions"!)

One of these was born on a Thanksgiving morning, when I was about six. My mother was preparing a grand Thanksgiving feast and was slightly behind in her cooking. I was called in from following my big brother around the house, and a tradition was born—the undeniably important task of making the cranberry sauce. If you've ever made cranberry sauce, you know that it's not that difficult, and the task therefore lent itself nicely to becoming the daughter's traditional Thanksgiving job.

A few years into this tradition, I served up a special batch of cranberry sauce. I had just turned eleven and was busy stirring the cranberries on the stove when I had a sudden urge to go to the bathroom. I yelled to whomever to come watch the cranberry sauce because I was dying to go. And with that, I was off.

I pulled down my pants and plopped down on the toilet. I was nearly approaching relief when I looked down into my underpants. There it was. But it didn't make any sense! I screamed out loud, "Mommeeeee . . . ! Is there any way the cranberry sauce could have gotten in my underwear?!" As I waited for her to answer me, I stared at it in horror, well aware that cranberry sauce stained.

"What?!" she yelled back, confused. I repeated my desperate question, and this time there was no answer. Instead she came running into the bathroom with our jolly Jamaican housekeeper in tow, with eyes wide open and sparkling. "That's not cranberry sauce!" Mom said. "That's your period. You've got your period!" The two of them stood directly in front of me, crammed into this tiny, cubicle-sized bathroom, and hovered over the evidence that was pulled down to my knees.

I looked at it again. "I have to go finish the cranberry sauce," I said and pulled up my pants to head back into the kitchen. They were at my heels.

"Honey! I can't believe it. You are so grown up. I'm so proud of you. . . . What are you doing?"

"Stirring," I said.

"Uh, um, well . . . actually, the cranberry sauce looks done to me. Let's turn off the stove and go to my bathroom so I can show you how to use a tampon," my mom offered.

I followed her to her bathroom.

She was strangely happy and eager about this, I thought, as she cleared off her perfume bottles from her mirrored tray and placed it on the floor in front of the toilet. She instructed me to stand over it, and she pointed at the mirror and explained everything I would need to know (and more). What I saw in the mirror was scary but sort of neat. There was a lot more to me than I had thought, but with her excellent explanation, it wasn't that difficult. Before I knew it, I had a little white string just like I had seen my mom have. It felt so grown up to be like her!

That evening at Thanksgiving dinner with all of our family and friends, my mom began the toast: "This year's cranberry sauce has even more tradition than any other year."

—Barclay Rachael Gang, Miami, FL

Barclay graduated with a bachelor of science in psychology from Tufts University and is currently pursuing her doctorate in neuropsychology in Miami.

Tsihabuhkai, 1962

Tsihabuhkai is the Comanche tribal word for *menses, menstrual, menstruate,* or *menstrual period.* That definition is far more than I knew at fourteen, when my first period arrived. My period was long overdue; most ninth-grade girls had their periods two years earlier, in the seventh grade. And I lied to my Central Junior High School friends who asked if I had my period. In addition to being self-conscious that I didn't have it yet, I felt that they openly discussed a topic that I felt was too private. In 1962, when I was fourteen, Comanche women rarely discussed personal matters such as periods; not with nonfamily and certainly not with those outside the culture.

My mother had not discussed the topic with me before my period came. She said, "I thought that your cousin told you all about it." She had also signed a school letter agreement when I was in the sixth grade giving the school nurse permission to discuss the topic with the girls. Who in the ninth grade remembers what they heard in class three years earlier? I certainly did not. I was ill-prepared for the changes in my life and my body the day my period arrived.

We had moved our house to a large Comanche allotment in the country that my father inherited from his uncle James Maddox. His uncle had neither married nor ever had children, but he was close to my father and left him land seven miles from Lawton, Oklahoma. I was in the ninth grade and thought my life was over. How would I see my friends? How could they visit me? We were leaving behind the Comanche Yellow Mission, a community of Comanche families and children. I knew everyone in the little Dutch Reformed Church community as my extended family. My father worked for the nearby Bureau of Indian Affairs' Soil and Moisture Conservation Agency, and my mother worked for the U.S. Public Health Service Indian Hospital as a seamstress. It was unusual in our community for a woman to work away from the home. And I was a "daddy's girl," although some might have described me as being a tomboy. I spent all of my free time with my father. We fished, went to movies, and worked in his wood shop together, so I was closer to him than to my mother. But everything changed when my period came.

Our transplanted house didn't yet have the electricity hooked up, and we used kerosene lamps. Our toilet was outdoors and some distance from our house. Of course, this would be the time when my long-overdue period would arrive! I remember sitting in the outhouse and feeling that something was not right. I checked my panties and saw the spot of blood. For a moment, I wondered if I was hurt—then I remembered. I smiled to myself—it was here. Finally, my period had come. I was normal after all. I cleaned up and ran to tell my mother. She seemed happy. She asked me what I knew. She seemed genuinely surprised at how little I was informed. She asked about the class and what they told me. I told her I couldn't remember anything. She helped me with the cumbersome pads and how to wear them and how to dispose of them with privacy and modesty. She told me of her own experience. It felt like my mother and I had a special and secret bond together. She told me, with a laugh, not to discuss it with my father. I felt closer to her than ever before. My mother told me that her period arrived during a parade in Walters, Oklahoma. She was riding a horse in the parade and wearing beautiful Comanche buckskin dress regalia. She was so embarrassed, and the dress was completely ruined! She told me that I was "lucky" to have had mine at home. After that time, I began spending less and less time with my father, doing the things that we did together, and more time with my mother.

131

Today, I am fifty-seven years old and once again, I don't have it. This is the story of my period, and I am sharing it with you because it is a new time. The arrival of our Tsihabuhkai is a special time—worthy of celebration.

—Juanita Pahdopony, Lawton, OK

Juanita is an enrolled member of Comanche Nation and an adjunct professor at the Comanche Nation College.

The Dream, 1994

I don't remember the first time I was informed about a period and what it entailed, but I do remember knowing for some time before my first bleed that it marked the physical capability of bearing children. This excited me because it made me feel older and more responsible.

I was attending Marin Waldorf School at the time of my first period. In addition to the school curriculum, the administration and faculty put on a "Coming-of-Age" festival, including parents and their children. At this festival, we discussed coming-of-age issues, such as menstrual cycles, etc. It was then that I was first introduced to cloth pads. Even though I obviously didn't know all the details of what a period was at that point in time, I fell in love! I loved the idea of having something to reuse as opposed to all the paper and plastic waste out there and felt empowered as a woman to make a positive difference in this area.

So one night, I had this incredible dream about becoming impregnated by some invisible force. I finally went into labor and had one baby . . . then another . . . and another . . . yet another . . . and finally another—five total! I was very impressed that my body could do such a thing, and then the babies just started popping out in an uncontrollable fashion with infinite numbers of babies. This so frightened me but excited me as well, to the point that I woke up only to discover that I was indeed sleeping in my very own blood from my very first period.

—Annie Sherman, Chico, CA

Annie Sherman grew up in Sonoma, California, and graduated from California State University, Chico, majoring in the social sciences. She was actively involved with the Women's Center on campus and is aspiring to make a career out of her passions—art, music, and helping people and the environment.

Operation Menstruation! 1998

It was the summer before entering high school and I was fourteen years old. My best friend, Sheena, and I felt like we were the last ones to get our periods; we were both anxious to finally become "women."

My mom had sat down with me years before to talk about my period and what it meant; it was a completely positive conversation. I learned that both she and my grandma had gotten theirs at around fourteen years of age, so I was patiently waiting.

Sheena and I had learned about tampons and maxi pads in our years of health class and had even practiced using them in anticipation of the big day. We very badly wanted to comment, as many of our friends did, about the comfort and convenience of these products, and so we waited.

Finally, it was the month before starting high school, and we were desperate.

What would we do in the changing room when girls were flaunting their tampons before our swim class or in health class when our friends described the excruciating pain that their menstrual cramps produced? We really *needed* to get our periods *now*!

We thought of a plan, although I don't know now whose idea it actually was.

My mom was taking the birth control pill, and we knew from our health classes that when you take the pills, you don't get your period, but when you stop taking them, voilà, your period arrives. Our plan was to discretely take out two pills from my mother's pack and each take one. We expected that a few days later, our periods would come. It was a perfect plan!

Finally, we gathered the courage to sneak into my mom's bathroom and search her drawers for the pills. She was at work for the day, and we had lots of time. But our plan sadly faltered. When we actually found the pills, we discovered that they were each assigned to a day of the week, and thus there was no way that we could take two without her noticing. We would have to enter high school as periodless girls.

A few months later, Sheena got her period, and I was alone waiting. It wasn't until three days before my fifteenth birthday that my period arrived—I was ecstatic. I was on cloud nine for a week afterward and proudly stored a box of tampons in my locker.

Years later I still remember how anxious we were and how excited I was when I finally became a "woman." I realize now that it actually had nothing to do with periods.

—Jennifer Asanin Dean, Hamilton, Canada

Jennifer was born and raised in Toronto and is currently a graduate student in the area of health geography at McMaster University. She eventually told her mom about her sleuthing adventures, and they can now laugh about it together.

Crushed Leaves in Kenya, 2006

The first time it happened, I was at home alone because my parents were at church. I was struck by a sudden pain in my abdomen. So I took some stomach-pain pills and lay down. Strangely, they didn't do anything, and I couldn't tell where the pain was coming from anymore. But when I went to the bathroom, I figured out what it was.

No one was home, so I had to deal with it all by myself. When my parents did get home, what irritated me was how concerned my mom was. Every twenty minutes, she kept asking me if I needed more pads and if I was okay. I'm okay, Mom. I'm a woman now. I know what to do.

I was lucky to buy pads. One thing that's different about periods in Kenya is that if you aren't middle or upper class, you don't go to school when you have your period because pads are so expensive. Girls will miss school for a week at a time, and if you miss school for that long everyone knows why. It makes girls want to go back to school even less at the end of the week. And it's so sad because no one does anything to help. Except there is this one guy who crushes plants and you put it in your underwear to help stop the bleeding. It actually works. I haven't tried it, though.

—Thatcher Mweu, Nairobi, Kenya

Thatcher plays softball, has a passion for 1990s boy bands, and had never seen a tampon before coming to study in the United States.

Editor's Note: When I started looking into what was being done about girls missing school in Africa, I discovered that there were a handful of nonprofit organizations working to address this problem. Some help by securing donations of sanitary supplies, others build more private toilets at girls' schools, and still others increase the number of women teachers who focus on health education. Please turn to Do More (page 199) for more information. Royalties from this book are helping to support the work of these organizations.

Where's My Belt? 1979

I clearly remember my first period. In spite of having read *Are You There God? It's Me, Margaret* by Judy Blume and having been warned repeatedly by my mother about it, I still thought I was dying when I pulled down my underwear and saw the rust-colored stain there (it was the rust color that confused me. It wasn't red. In books it's always red).

I was in my girlfriend Laura's bathroom (it was the morning after an overnight stay), so it wasn't like I could yell for my mom to come look. I got out of there as fast as I could (I couldn't tell Laura because she was only in fifth grade and I was in sixth grade, and I knew she was too young to be told her best friend was dying) and managed to make it out of her house without crying, though I cried the whole way home (which was across the street).

When I got to my house and told my mom, she very calmly examined the stain and said it was my period (even though I insisted it wasn't because it wasn't red). Then she handed me a pad, the kind with the peel-off, stick-on backing, which I then insisted was the wrong kind, because in *Are You There God? It's Me, Margaret*, they had the kind you attach to belts you wear around your waist.

So then my mom had to explain that the book I'd read was a little out of date and they didn't make maxi pads for belts anymore, but if it was that important to me, we could go look for some, but it was much easier to stick them on the bottom of your panties. I remember feeling totally scammed because I actually wanted to wear a belt under my clothes for some reason. I was a very weird kid.

The one thing that mortified me the most was that none of my friends had had their periods yet, so I felt like a freak and felt like I couldn't talk about it with anyone. Not anyone (except my mom, but that was too embarrassing)!

Also tampons freaked me out, even though my mom kept pushing them on me. It took me a year before I got the guts to try them, so no swimming for me during the summer if I was having my period, and also I skipped ballet during my period.

And I also wouldn't carry pads around with me to school for the first year I had my period because I didn't own a purse or even a backpack and even if I had, I didn't want to admit I needed them. It seems amazing to me when I think back on this, but I would wear the same pad for the whole day. (Yuck! My mom never caught on.)

Finally I saw an eighth grader and president of the student council, Jill, walk up to the tampon machine in the girls' room and buy a tampon for ten cents because she'd gotten her period at school. She turned the crank, looked at me, and went, "Doesn't getting your period at school suck?" or something like that and went back to her stall.

After that, I realized it wasn't something to be embarrassed of or secretive about. Also that you could *buy* pads and tampons at school. So I started doing that. Also I thought Jill was the coolest girl I had ever seen, even when a huge scandal broke out among the girls in my class about her and the fact that her tampon string was *showing* out the side of her bikini bottom during a cheerleading car wash fund-raiser. I thought, *So what?* We all wore tampons. Even, by that time, me.

Although it wasn't until another overnight the following summer with all my best friends that three of them revealed they'd gotten their periods, too, and only my very best friend hadn't, that I finally felt comfortable enough to talk about periods openly with my friends. We made up a secret name for our periods—"shells," because that was the symbol on the tampon machine—which is incredibly stupid, but it made us laugh like crazy. Except for our friend who hadn't had hers. She got mad and rolled over and went to sleep. We tried to tell her she was overreacting and that having your period wasn't so great. And it isn't. Except now I realize it kind of is.

—Meg Cabot, Bloomington, IN

Meg Cabot is the author of more than fifty books, including the best-selling Princess Diaries series. Meg explains that her work's overarching theme is that her readers "are not alone in feeling the way I did when I was in middle and high school— like a great big freak! Also that 'normal' is not what you see on TV."

My Second First Period, 1977

I sat under the wooden awning that covered the lunch tables on the schoolyard, watching the gate and praying. It was 3:15 on a bright April afternoon and the final bell had just rung. Most of the kids made their way out of the gate, carrying Partridge Family lunch boxes, joking with each other, and racing. I sat at the table and solemnly watched the entrance, scrutinizing every figure who approached. Today, all the girls in fifth grade had been asked to stay and watch a movie with their mothers. During the week, the upcoming film had been the main topic of gossip among us girls. I knew what was coming, and as I sat, counting one by one as my classmates' mothers arrived, I wished the movie and its inherent self-consciousness was the only thing I had to be concerned about.

I studied the women breezing through the school gate and tried to imagine what it would be like to have a mother who dressed in bell-bottom slacks with colorful blouses and long, crocheted vests, like that one. Or better yet, those faux-patched hip-hugger jeans, a wide vinyl belt around a trim waist, and Dr. Scholl's sandals on tanned feet. Or that mom, with lots of long, streaked hair and silver jewelry, pale lipstick.

After a time, the stream of mothers lessened to a trickle. Mine wasn't among the stragglers. Mrs. Vernon, the fifth-grade teacher, came out and called the twitchy group of mothers and daughters inside to start the meeting. I sighed low, off the hook. Sure, I wished I had a regular mother to attend school functions so I didn't feel so out of place, but I certainly didn't want it to be my mother. Turning to walk up the concrete stairs that led to the nearly deserted hallway, I looked back at the gate one last time. When I recognized the short, stout, harried woman rushing toward the gate, my solar plexus turned to lead.

She was wearing her best muumuu, the one with the fluo-rescent yellow and fuchsia orchids, woven flip-flops on her feet exposing long, hoary toenails. Dark rouge stood out against her pale, powdery cheeks, and her bloodred lipstick was chalky. Her hair, dyed a brassy shade of orange, was not fixed in any discernible style but was held in place with Aqua Net hair spray, the scent of which could be picked up a dozen feet away. A dirty beige handbag was slung over her shoulder, a purse that I knew was littered with bits of tobacco and old eyebrow pencils. My mother seemed relatively balanced, though I knew I wasn't the best judge of that. Anytime my mother was dressed and out of bed, she seemed relatively okay to me.

"Yoo-hoo," my mother waved. The too-loud voice, thick with that attention-seizing Irish brogue, carried across the playground. For half an instant, I hoped that Mrs. Vernon wouldn't notice the late arrival and I could slip in without my mother noticing. Maybe then she'd give up and go back home.

"One moment, girls." Mrs. Vernon held up the group. "We have one more mother coming."

Walking into the school auditorium, I tried to steer my mother to a seat in the back corner and hoped the film and the ensuing darkness would start immediately. I discreetly checked her for potential danger signs: the sound of her voice indicated the influence of countless psychotropic drugs, but her words weren't slurred and her hands weren't shaking.

There wasn't much I remembered about the film and the following question-and-answer session except the desire to disappear, to be wiped off the face of the earth. My mother tried to make conversation with the other moms there, mothers I knew from Girl Scouts and field trips, women my own mother had never met.

After that period film, my mother took it as a sign of progressiveness that she could discuss these "woman things" so openly. On days when she was feeling good, she'd talk in glowing terms of menstruation.

"It's a wonderful rite of passage. Nothing to be afraid of," she said encouragingly. Under her breath I heard her mumble, "Wish someone had taken the time to talk to me." And then in a louder voice, "But, no matter . . . you'll become a full-fledged woman, capable of bearing children. You'll join the ranks of womanhood once and for all." My mother was more excited by the prospect of womanhood than I was.

The big day arrived when I was fourteen years old and in eighth grade. My mother was in the state mental institution in Camarillo, trying electroshock for the third time. The first two attempts apparently didn't take.

Covertly, I looked through my mother's things in the bathroom cupboard and found the large box of bulky Kotex pads. I knew what to do with them. Throughout the week, I carefully hid the used pads under piles of waste in the alleyway trash cans. I never told my father. Coming home from school the day before my mother was expected to return, I bought a replacement box of pads with my allowance; Mom would never know the difference.

My mother slowly resumed her remote role in the family, rather like a ghost whose presence or absence changed the mood of the place but whose countenance could not be seen. She was in bed, cushioned from the world by her stained bathrobe and pill bottles, a few weeks later when I called out to her from the bathroom.

"Mom," I yelled, "come here." By the time she made her way to my voice, I'd arranged my face into a look of shock and surprise. "Look! I've started my period."

"Oh, honey," she gushed, holding on to the doorframe for support. "This is so special. Your very first period! Let me show you what to do."

I watched patiently as she demonstrated the placement of pads, how to dispose of them, what to do for cramps.

"It won't be so traumatic next time," she assured me.

By my next period, I'd figured out how to use tampons and had bought a razor to master my unsightly underarm growth, another thing Mom never thought to address. But I let her think she'd been an exemplary mother. If I were found out—about the surreptitiously bought bra, the tampons, the razor—my mother would see these actions as a rebuke. And I knew what usually followed that: another trip to Camarillo, more responsibility for my younger siblings foisted onto my shoulders, another situation for me to amend.

—Bernadette Murphy, Los Angeles, CA

Bernadette is the author of three books, including Zen and the Art of Knitting; *she teaches creative writing at Antioch University's MFA program and is working on* Grace Notes, *a novel about music, motherhood, and madness.*

Memory: Day 1, 1973

My father spread out his arms as if drawing back a veil.
"Do you like it?" he asked,
a cigar hanging from his lips. His artist's hands clasped
tightly after clapping
their satisfaction. "Something your Old Man made for you.
You can take it with you
to college. When you get big."

My mother disappeared between a clanking pot and boiling
water. "I must tell him,"
she had said when I showed her the pad, and excitedly
picked up the phone to dial.
"Your daughter is a woman today," she whispered, a small
joy in her voice as they
shared my secret.

Later, he arrived home with a box, grinning as if the thing
he carried was magic.
I listened to his alternate cursing and banging for hours
until the sound
of socks sliding over perfectly sanded wood replaced his
voice.
He walked slowly from the bedroom and called my name twice,
gently laughing.
As he spread his arms, he stepped aside to reveal oak so
solid the tree could have grown

in the corner and invited him to carve it. Loving me, he accepted the offer, unashamed and unafraid to reveal his own imperfections. The top drawer hung lower to the left. A brass knob was crookedly screwed into the second drawer.

I walked toward the bulk that hid my father's true calling of oil and charcoal on canvas. He had polished the wood to a brilliance. "It was on sale," he said. "Not perfect. But, not bad. When you get big, maybe you'll remember me." He breathed deeply. "You're a woman now. But don't forget, you'll always be my daughter."

—M. Eliza Hamilton Abegunde, Evanston, IL   145

Abegunde is a Cave Canem fellow and the author of Wishful Thinking, Still Breathing, *and* What Is Now Unanswerable. *Her work appears in journals, including the* Kenyon Review, RHINO, *and* nocturnes, *and is anthologized in* I Feel a Little Jumpy Around You, Knowing Stones: Poems of Exotic Places, Beyond the Frontier, Catch the Fire, *and* Jane's Stories II. *She is an advisory board member for* RHINO. *This poem is from a collection in process,* My Father's Hands.

A Coup at the Napkin Dispenser, 1960

It could not have been a more confusing time for me. My best friend was somewhere in Havana—a quick and popular excursion for Floridians. Her father, then mayor of

Miami, had taken his family there to celebrate New Year's 1960. Suddenly there was word of a coup as the dictator, Fulgencio Batista, was overthrown by the young revolutionary Fidel Castro. American tourists were holed up in their hotels while bullets whistled through the streets. This was the backdrop for my first menses.

Returning safely, my friend's vacation story was far more dramatic than mine—hers as a witness to history while mine was elemental and inevitable. I had been prepared for the arrival of menarche by a film I saw in school, and my mother had also given me a book to read. She provided me with what felt like gigantic and uncomfortable padding and an elastic harness. This mattress between my legs prevented me from walking straight, and I soon understood that tampons must have been invented for us Florida girls, whose bikini bottoms were attached to the mouths of puppies on the Coppertone billboards all over town.

But I would still have my own moment to be center stage. Two months later, uprooted from my natal home and my best friend, my family relocated to Springfield, New Jersey. Much to the distress of my mother and I, my father had accepted an upper-level job with a pharmaceutical company. My third period found me in the girls' locker room of a junior high school as my new friends, Nancy, Andrea, Anita, Roni, Roberta, and Pam, watched with astonishment as I (the new girl) calmly went to the wall and placed a nickel in the sanitary-napkin dispenser. I smiled as I looked at their openmouthed surprise. I was the first in this new group of friends to need Kotex, and by virtue of that, my position was assured.

—Linda Lindroth, New Haven, CT

Linda is a photographer, independent curator, and coauthor of Virtual Vintage: The Insider's Guide to Buying and Selling Fashion Online. *She is an adjunct professor of visual culture at Quinnipiac University.*

Downward Dog, 2004

My parents have always believed that knowledge is power. They were never afraid to use big words around me and were sure to answer my many questions in a complete manner—usually with a list of books I could go to if I wanted even more information. So it was entirely typical that when I started growing mosquito bites and finding hair in funny places, they would kit me out with my own library of "owner's manuals." I soon was very well read on the subjects of bra fitting and "menstruntan." (I was confounded for years by the proper pronunciation, as well as with that of the "public" area.) After studying the drawings of the vagina and uterus, I felt well prepared for my supposed first steps into womanhood.

But my period didn't come then. It may have been that all my friends got theirs particularly young, or because I was among the younger girls in the grade, but I soon felt that I was the only girl in the entire world who didn't have hers. And the longer it took to come, the more my mother felt compelled to talk about it. I can't even count the number of times she explained the risk of toxic shock syndrome (which she herself had suffered from) or the intricacies of tampon disposal. If my eye rolls were too obvious, she would remind me of the experience of my great-grandmother. Growing up in a different time and place, one wouldn't have discussed such things. Ever. When her period finally arrived, she fell to pieces in the fear that she was dying. (At that point, I would usually reach over and turn up the volume dial on the radio.)

Yet even with the visual aids, the family history, the preemptive tampon practice, it seemed that nothing would coax my period into arriving. Nothing, that is, except for *adho mukha savasana*—the downward-facing dog pose. As I worked my way through my sun-salute warm-ups one morning at theater camp, I felt my stomach cramp painfully. I ignored it, thinking I had tweaked an abdominal muscle. And later, when I went to the bathroom and found my underwear a rusty brown, my first instinct was that I had had an accident in my pants! Even after all that research and waiting, I was completely blind to the fact that I had gotten my period. Steps into womanhood, indeed!

—Marian Firke, Chicago, IL

Marian is a very flexible high school student. Although she still practices yoga on occasion, she prefers theater and dance.

The Harness, 1961

When the first spots of blood appeared on my underpants, I shyly slipped into the kitchen and whispered to my mother. She told me to go into the bathroom and she would meet me there. I waited for a few minutes and then she opened the door, closed it conspiratorially behind her, and handed me a gray and bloodstained menstrual belt and a sanitary pad. The belt was stretched out from years of wear (my mother was a large woman), and she adjusted it to fit my thirteen-year-old skinny waist. She gave me brief instructions, then left the room in embarrassment.

I struggled awkwardly into the belt and pad, feeling humiliated and ugly when I looked into the mirror. I remember thinking, "This is a woman's harness." I began to sob with my lost girlhood and with the legacy of shame my mother bestowed upon me that day.

—Deo Robbins, Santa Cruz, CA

Deo Robbins is a fifty-six-year-old grandmother of identical twin toddlers, whom she is helping to raise in their three-generation household. She is the cofounder (with her husband, author John Robbins) of EarthSave International.

The Von Trapps and Me, 1980

When I started the sixth grade, I didn't think too much about which girls in my class had gotten their periods. I'd read all of Judy Blume's books, so I was pretty confident that I knew all I needed to know about getting my first period, and I was in no hurry to have to personally deal with something that just seemed like a big, gross nuisance. I also thought getting your period seemed like something you should keep secret. Not that it was a shameful thing or anything like that, but that maybe it was impolite to talk about it. Like farts. Everyone does them but it's rude to talk about them. But I found out this wasn't true for everyone when my best friend, Jenny, told me that she longed to be able to ask the other girls in our class for nickels when she was in the girls' bathroom.

"Why?" I asked.

"Because then they'll know that *I* am a woman, *too*," she said, rolling her eyes extravagantly at me, "duh-uh."

"Oh, right," I remember saying, but I didn't get what she meant until a few hours later, when I noticed that the sanitary-napkin machine in the girls' bathroom had a nickel slot.

I never wanted to ask anyone for a nickel. I didn't even want my mother to talk to me about periods. Ever. Especially not around my brother or father. When she tried to bring the subject up one time after breakfast, I glared at her. Then I pretended to be engrossed in reading my horoscope in the paper.

I first got my period while watching *The Sound of Music* on TV. It was a Friday night and I was staying at my grandmother's house. It was the first time I had ever seen that movie and I had been really enjoying the first half hour. At thirteen, part of me was embarrassed that I still loved movies like this. I secretly watched Laura Ingalls deal with her life in Walnut Grove every Monday night. I had learned earlier that year that this was not a well-respected activity when I'd written *Little House on the Prairie* as "My Favorite TV Show" in a slambook. Slambooks are passed around the class for everyone to fill out and read each other's entries. After the other kids read the slambook, I was constantly teased because my pick was a "baby show." The fact that I had entered Air Supply as "My Favorite Rock Band" didn't help advance my cool status any, either.

Thank God the night I got my first period, my father and brother weren't with me. They were staying at our family's newly built cabin, up on top of a nearby mountain about fifteen minutes away from my grandparents' house. I can't believe I am about to say this, but I was so grateful for my cramps because I had mistaken them for the stomach flu that afternoon. If I hadn't had them, my mom and I would have gone up to the cabin, too. I shudder to think that I would have gotten my first period as Laura Ingalls must have gotten hers, in a one-room log cabin with no running water. There was nothing charming about that idea to me.

When I went to the bathroom during a commercial break in *The Sound of Music*'s broadcast and discovered the blood, I wasn't scared; I was irritated. I felt inconvenienced. What a horrible time to have to deal with this mess. My grandmother didn't have anything in her cupboards that I could use. I considered just shoving some toilet paper in my pants but was afraid what might happen if I bled through that and soiled my grandmother's couch or afghan. I didn't know how to bring it up to my mother. Even though I didn't want to tell her, I knew I had to. It was just that my mother could be so dramatic at times, like when I got my first bra, she had to tell the saleslady about it with such pride in her voice. I wanted to kick her. I dreaded having to hear about the watershed characteristics of this great event. My mom used lots of big words, like "watershed," because she used to be an English teacher.

I was grateful that when I did call her into the bathroom to tell her what was going on, she was very low key about it. She asked me if I had any questions and I told her no. I told her I just wanted to get back to the TV to find out what Maria and the Von Trapp kids were up to. After showing me how to adhere a pad to my underpants, my mom left me alone in the bathroom to change. I was disappointed when I got back to the movie and found out things with *The Sound of Music* had also changed while I'd been away. And not for the better.

I didn't get why Maria couldn't stay a wacky nun and just hang out, playing and singing with the pretty Von Trapp kids. I couldn't understand why Maria was flirting with that sourpuss father, Captain Von Trapp. And I especially couldn't comprehend why the stupid Nazis were trying to ruin everything. Now the whole family had to leave the home they'd loved so much. Why couldn't everyone just stay carefree and silly? Why did everything need to move on and be different? I crossed my arms over my chest, wishing I could just make things stay the same. Fun and happy. Without periods or Nazis to complicate things.

—Debby Dodds, Los Angeles, CA

Debby "likes to amuse people whenever possible," which explains why she was featured in the Women in Comedy Festival at the Laugh Lounge in New York City. She has written a screenplay called Whackjob *and coauthored several plays, including the box-office hit* Girls on the Edge, *as well as several stage shows for Disneyland. Her work has been published in* Hip Mama, Sun *magazine, the* Crimson Crane, *and* Zinkzine.com.

Dress Appropriately, 1974

There was nothing extraordinary about when and where my period started. I was twelve. It started during the last period at school, but there was no embarrassment because I was wearing our school uniform, navy blue pants. I was comforted by my grandmother's assurance that having periods is a minor nuisance in these modern days of factory-made disposable pads—in her day, she said to my horror, they had stacks of homemade cloth napkins that had to be hand washed.

What was extraordinary about having periods for me,

which took a few months after the first period to sink in, was how much it would change my life, for good and for bad. I was angry for months, if not years, about having periods. It reminded me, it still reminds me, that I am a female in a society, in a world, that discriminates against women.

When I was twelve, I was a tomboy going to one of the few coed schools in Tehran. I spent school recess playing basketball or Ping-Pong with boys. I was better than most of them, so I felt like their equal. I was in denial. But the periods kept coming every month, reminding me that I would not be seen on their level. The denial had to stop. After a while, my anger was replaced with the strong sense that I simply had to work harder to be considered their equal. That was the good change. The bad change was—and is—the sheer inconvenience of bleeding for almost a week every month. After thirty years, I still cannot get used to it. You have to stash tampons and pads everywhere, just in case. You have to avoid wearing that favorite cream linen skirt for a week every month. You have to watch what you eat so you don't get anemic. And no matter how prepared you are, disasters keep happening.

Two years ago, I was in Berlin attending an international conference. My period started a couple of days early and very heavily in the middle of a scientific session. Who cared that it was important for my career to stay in that session and take part in the discussion—I had to dash out to the bathroom to use the one tampon I always have with me and then run out and jump in a cab to take me to

154

my hotel room, where I had my ample supply of pads and tampons that I never leave the country without. Thankfully, this being Germany, I was wearing black. But what if this had happened a few months earlier, at another high-profile conference in San Diego, when I was wearing that cream skirt?

I had the period talk with my nine-year-old daughter several months ago. She listened intently and only had one question for me: "Does this happen to boys?" "No," I said. Without hesitation, she said with outrage, "But that is not fair!" I couldn't agree more, I told her. What getting periods teaches you is that life will not be fair; it will be full of nuisances and disasters. But you can handle it, as long as you know what to wear.

—Bita Moghaddam, Pittsburgh, PA

Bita is a professor of neuroscience at the University of Pittsburgh.

The Earache, 1975

I was fifteen and wondering when it was going to happen. My mom figured that I had learned about it at school, so she never spoke to me about it. One day I came down with a really bad earache in my right ear. It hurt so bad that I went to see the family doctor in the middle of the day. When I came back, I had really bad cramps and went to the bathroom. When I saw the blood, I was so unused to the sight that I passed out and ended up on the floor. When I told my mom the news, she handed me a Kotex box. I remember that I then said, "I don't think so . . . ," and she went out to get a box of tampons.

It was common for me to pass out in the early days of my period. I think it happened about three times a year. About six years later, I recall getting a really bad earache, and again, it turned out to happen on the day that I got my period. In time, and after having three kids, periods stopped being so complicated.

—Dr. Miriam Nelson, Medford, MA

Mim is a women's health advocate and best-selling author of the Strong Women book series. She serves as director of the John Hancock Center for Physical Activity and Nutrition at Tufts University.

Progressive Parenting, 1993

Of course, feminist families carry none of the baggage other families have about sex and the body. Feminist children grow up embracing their emerging sexuality, always strong, self-loving, and confident in their corporal selves.

And, if you'll just sign right here, we'll be happy to sell you the Brooklyn Bridge.

First, let's set the scene: two parents, raised Catholic, absorbing stereotypical repression of both sexuality and body awareness. In Mom's family, eating (or not eating) was the response to both good and bad feelings, and women's traditional physical attractiveness was highly valued. Dad comes from a family where the "birds and bees" talk was two sentences long and clear as mud. But, having discovered feminism, we thought it would be pretty easy to slice right through those silly old ways and do better in raising our twin daughters.

In actuality, we did more muddling than slicing, doing some things well, some poorly, and some just plain hilariously.

To start with, our girls were pretty and got regular comments from family and strangers about their appearance. So we zealously praised their bodies for what they could do, not how they looked. We practically made a religion of never commenting on their weight or size (or ours) when they were around. We even threw out the bathroom scale because Mom didn't want to pass on her habit of self-judging by the pound. As it turned out, Nia's and Mavis's biggest body anxiety was "I'm too short." ("Quick! What famous women are short?")

With sexuality, things were just a tad more complicated. But we still clung to the delusion that our highly developed feminist sensibilities would make everything easy. When the girls were eleven, we all launched *New Moon* magazine together, putting in articles about rites of passage and celebrating menarche. We figured it was a cinch that each daughter would rejoice in her first period, proudly trumpeting its arrival as a sign of her feminine strength and the perfect occasion to throw a party.

Not quite. The big event was announced with a whisper, not a whoopee. "Come in here, Mom, and shut the door. I think I'm having my period. Promise you won't tell Dad and, jeez, no rite-of-passage party, okay?"

We did eventually celebrate, but not as we'd imagined. Mom treated each girl to a mother-daughter dinner out. It was a little trickier for Dad. He consistently wins the "worst-at-keeping-secrets" prize but managed to play along this time, never letting on that he knew about the Moon Goddess's visits. About a year later, he got his chance to celebrate. Heading out to the Super Valu, he shouted, "Need anything at the store?"

"Can you get me some pads?" called a teenage voice. "I'm out."

He waited until the door shut before dancing down the driveway whispering, "*Yessss!!!* She finally told me!"

Over the years, Mom imparted lots of other basic information with minimal angst. At one point, she decided it was time for a purely practical conversation, focusing on contraception, STD prevention, and myths about sex. She anticipated a receptive, even appreciative audience for the demonstration of how to put a condom on a zucchini, use a dental dam, etc. The "talk" managed to both insult and scare the first daughter. With such an unsuccessful launch, Nancy dreaded "talk #2" even more than the first, but the girls got the essential information and we all lived through it.

Some of us claim we don't even remember certain parts of all this. Still, we can all laugh about it. And the messages seem to have been communicated, absorbed, and used. ("Used?! You mean they might actually have sex someday?" "Calm down, dear.") We had crossed the treacherous waters, at least for now, and we didn't even have to sell off the Brooklyn Bridge.

—Nancy Gruver and Joe Kelly, Duluth, MN

Nancy Gruver is the founder of New Moon Girl Media (www .newmoongirls.com), which provides an online community for girls ages 8–15 and publishes the bimonthly magazine New Moon Girls. *Joe Kelly is the author of the best seller* Dads and Daughters: How to Inspire, Support and Understand Your Daughter *(www.dadsanddaughters.com).*

Showdown at the HoJo, 1968

We were just coming back from a year in Rome, where my father had decided to take his Fulbright . . . and the rest of his family. I was twelve years old at the time. It was a dreadful year for me. Uprooted from my friends, I was planted in an Italian public school where, for the second time in my young life, I was expected to not just speak Italian but function in Italian as if I were a native. I felt stupid. My body was changing. Despite my protestations, my mother had my hair cut very short. I felt fat and ugly. I envied my little sister's (three years my junior) ability to eat whatever she wanted and still look like a little kid.

We took a boat back to the States and then made the trip by car from New York City back to Chicago. The road trip highlights were always rest stops and swimming pools. On the first day of the drive home, I had excruciating pains in my stomach. I felt like someone was twisting my insides, and I insisted that we stop as soon as possible. It turned out to be at that oasis of American culture—Howard Johnson's. I went to the bathroom and screamed when I saw the blood streaming down my legs. I fainted, my mother called my father into the bathroom, and so it began. I'm not sure what was worse: thinking that I was dying or wanting to die because my father was in the women's bathroom, commenting and hopelessly trying to be helpful.

Perhaps I missed the sex education I would have received had I still been in the States that year. Perhaps my mother was planning to say something to me about menstruation. Perhaps she felt uncomfortable with the whole subject because of how her mother had handled it with her. At that moment, I made a conscious decision that my daughter would have a very different experience.

—Linda Greenberg, Chicago, IL

Linda received a Ph.D. in cultural anthropology from the University of Chicago and runs a marketing research firm. With two friends, she recently started Via Mia Design—an Italian-inspired jewelry company producing one-of-a-kind, wearable pieces of art.

No Longer in Little League, 1993

I got my first period in sixth grade at age twelve. I was well aware that it would arrive someday. However, I was not expecting it to be the afternoon prior to a softball game. My mother supplied me with a *huge* pad, or so I felt at the time, that I knew everyone would be able to see under my softball pants. The pants were not spandex tight, but I felt the bulge was enormous and highly visible. My mom assured me no one would notice. I was a pitcher for the team and therefore the center of attention for most of the game. No one ever said anything, but to this day, I swear it was noticed by *everyone* in the crowd. I stopped using pads after that.

—Moira Kathleen Ray, Portland, OR

Moira is a left-handed nature lover. She is currently training to become a physician.

Euro Disney, 1992

My first menstruation happened in a perfect world. When I say "perfect world," I mean it. I was at Disney World, Paris! I was twelve years old and inside the "Walt Disney's Princess World" bathroom. Everyone was outside waiting for me because they wanted to go on the newest ride, Space Mountain. I opened the door of the white and pink bathroom, and I sat down to pee. I looked at my panties and was horrified. I was a tomboy, and this blood was a symbol of everything I hated about being a girl. I started thinking about a previous conversation with my mother about becoming a woman and being able to have children . . . but why now? And in the middle of the most wonderful family vacation? I wanted to stop the bleeding, so I finally convinced myself to call my older sister.

I tried opening the door, but it was stuck. My face turned blue; I started panicking and knocking on the door, hoping that someone else was in the bathroom. I guess that being the first one in the park at 8:00 a.m. was not an advantage at this point anymore. I was bloody, scared, alone, and helpless in the Disney World bathroom! After five minutes of sobbing, I decided to crawl underneath the bathroom door. Thank God I was a skinny teenager! I could smell the Clorox from the floor, but the only thought on my mind was getting help.

I came outside, where everyone was already complaining about how much time I was making them all waste, and it got even worse when I asked my sister to come back with me into the bathroom. They all looked at me like I was crazy. My father was impatient and yelling, and my brother and little sister were wondering if I had diarrhea. I went back inside with my sister and explained my problem. She stopped being mad at me and gave me a small tampon that she had in her backpack. It was so easy to put in that I started to worry that it might get lost inside me because I could not feel it. But all trace of anxiety and panic attack went away as I waited in line for the different rides. It wasn't till four hours later, when my sister gently reminded me, that I went to change my tampon. No one else ever knew what really happened to me that day, and it was only this year that I finally told my father when my first period was. From that whole vacation, the pink and white bathroom was the scariest ride I experienced!

—Jessy Schuster, Miami, FL

Jessy was born in France and lived in Guadeloupe for fifteen years. She arrived in Miami in 1999 and has been living there ever since. She is a student at Miami Dade College studying journalism and mass communication. She is also working for the Haitian Television Network as the host of an entertainment program called En Vogue, *where she interviews artists (musicians, singers, actors) and covers different events and festivals in Miami.*

On Horseback, 1960s

I was always a terrible tomboy and precocious as well. Around the age of nine, I became aware of those large boxes of Kotex in the house. Though I'm not sure where I learned what they were for, I am sure of what I did with the information. I tortured Mother, asking what they were for. Dusting, perhaps? I enjoyed her discomfort and her "I'll tell you later" rejoinders. Maybe a year later, I was riding and put my horse to a three-foot jump called a chicken coop. The horse refused, and I cartwheeled in the air. From straddling the horse, I ended up straddling the chicken coop. Later in the afternoon, I had to go to the bathroom and headed for some bushes. I saw a little blood on my panties and rushed home to tell my mother that "I had become a woman." She just laughed at me. I always say I lost my virginity to a chicken coop.

My first period came somewhat later, I think in the seventh grade. Mother and I had had our talk. I recall having cramps and not being surprised but walking cross-legged the rest of the day. And taking frequent bathroom breaks to check that it was really happening. This time when I told my mother, she believed me and lightly slapped my face.

Some tribe or another believes that when you get your period, there is a moment when you can see the crack in the world. Sometimes it is just a chocolate craving! I've always liked the phrase "I'm in my moon."

—Margaret Whitton, Martha's Vineyard, MA

Margaret is a stage and screen actress whose credits include Major League, The Man Without a Face, Mr. Baseball, *and* The Tempest, *in Shakespeare in the Park at the Delacorte Theater. She is also a theater director and writes a column about baseball.*

Not Getting It, 1980

What I remember most about getting my period is not getting it.

And not getting it. And not getting it.

I just could not get the thing, no matter how many white bikinis I wore, even on boats, without bringing a pad along just in case; no matter how many phantom cramps I willed into my uterus. Nothing.

What I got instead was strep throat.

I was regular my whole seventh-grade year, more regular in my monthly affliction than even my most developed friends were in theirs: once a month, every month that year, I would wake up with what felt like a tennis ball lodged in my throat. The pink stuff flowed for me every month, just like for all the other girls, only mine was erythromycin.

It felt like a poor substitute.

It felt like a mockery.

Hello, body? Wrong area! My body clearly didn't know how to do it, the whole growing-up thing; it was confused, dopey, slow. While all my friends were heading to the drugstore on their own, buying supplies for their mature bodies, I was once again huddled, feverish and small, between my mom and the burbling fish tank at the pediatrician's office, declining to play with the stacking toys or the drooly little kids who were apparently my real peers.

But on a sleepover at my new best friend Bea's house, we

confessed the truth to each other: *No, never got it, at least, not yet. You either?* What a relief. *Do you get strep throat every month? No, why? Oh,* I retreated. *Just wondering.*

It was a bond, though. It seemed like everybody else had matured beyond us. "I haven't become a woman yet," we said and giggled crazily. *Woman woman woman,* what a silly-sounding word. It felt foreign in our mouths, like nonsense, like nothing to do with us. Woman? No way. Okay, then, if we were the only ones left in the land of the little kids, well, at least we were there together.

But we both knew that the day would come when one of us would get it. The other would be left behind. Would it tear us apart? Would the shift break the bonds of intimacy and shared immaturity, so newly formed?

We decided strict honesty would be our way, and swore to tell each other the instant it happened—no delays, no secrets from each other. We wouldn't let worry seep in; we were best friends and if one of us got it, it meant we were both on our way. And telling each other immediately would be our way to cement our bond.

Since we were going to be apart (at different sleep-away camps) for the potentially huge summer between seventh and eighth grades, we wrote letters to each other in advance, together, to be mailed the minute after either of us got our period. Each letter was written by both of us, alternating letters, so that it would be a shared experience even if in some ways it could never be. Each letter said simply:

And was signed with a *, our secret symbol for ourselves together.

We each went to camp with the special letter tucked among our sweatshirts and socks, our sealed maxi-pad boxes and unnecessary AAA bras.

The days ticked by without any reason to send my letter, and while I partly hoped that one of us would get it even if it had to be Bea, I had to admit to some relief that her letter never arrived.

We both eventually got our periods, not over the summer but during the school year, so we never sent our letters after all. Neither of us now remembers which of us got her period first, I guess because it mattered less and less to us. We knew our friendship could handle it, that our solidarity went deeper than what we lacked in hormonal upheaval. I knew if she got hers first, she would tell me, share it with me, tell me the details and the truth about everything she felt, and that if I got mine first, she would want to know everything and celebrate with me.

I actually don't remember much about finally getting mine at all (though I remember I got strep throat much less frequently). I do know it felt good to think my body was actually finally figuring out what to do, and that even if it took its own sweet time, I could trust it to get there eventually.

But before I learned to trust my body, I had learned to trust my friend.

So maybe I had become a woman already.

—Rachel Vail, New York, NY

Growing up, Rachel couldn't decide whether to become an actress, financial wizard, lobbyist, magician, playwright, or spy. She ultimately found a way to combine them all by becoming a writer. Her novels for teens include If We Kiss, Lucky, *and* Gorgeous. *She has written more than a dozen children's books as well, including* Sometimes I'm Bombaloo *and* Jibberwillies at Night.

The Mermaid, 1974

So here I am, at the top of the stairs, screaming, "Mom! Mom!" in a slightly hysterical, somewhat delirious state of mind. My mom finally appears: she is wiping her hands on a dish towel.

"What?" she asks from the bottom of the stairs, looking up.

"There's something in my underwear."

Suddenly, my mom looks like she is going to jump into a jig. She brightens up, smiling some silly smile, and it seems to me she is now much younger, as if she has turned into a teenager, not much older than me.

"It's started!" She gleams.

"It has?" I ask.

"Yes, your period! How *exciting*!!" Now she looks to be positively glowing, and I am caught up in her joy. This seems to be a good thing, this bleeding that has begun.

Later that day, I tell her I want to go swimming. She tells me I'll need to insert a tampon.

I spend the next two hours upstairs, reading the instructions, trying over and over to plunge that hard cotton wad up into my twassy. Finally, I get one in the middle and up inside. Now I have to go lie down on a bed. I feel sick. I feel like I have had twenty shots of tequila (although at the time I couldn't know that that is what I would later be comparing the sensation to . . . being drunk). Having something *inside* me is unnerving, unnatural.

I am reeling and lie down. I think: Good God, all this to go swimming?! When did swimming become so important? And then the fear: what if I go swimming and the tampon floats out?

I have never forgotten my first period. I have to credit my mom for making it a memory so easy to recall. And, just to let you know, I did go swimming, and the tampon didn't fall out. I pretended I was a mermaid and let the cool water glide over my new, sleek body: a woman's body.

—Sara Hickman, Austin, TX

Sara is a mom, musician, and self-described creative elf. Performing Songwriter *magazine calls her one of the top 100 most influential independent artists of the past fifteen years.*

When you phoned home from California to tell me it had started

A brilliant globule of blood
rolled out over the surface of the desert
up and down the Continental Divide
through the singing prairies
parting the Mississippi
leaping the Delaware Water Gap
until it spilled into this tall red kitchen
in Rocky Hill, New Jersey
where it skittered across the linoleum
and cracked into hundreds of little faceted jewels.

I will not diminish this day with labeling
I will not say foolishly
"now you are a woman"
I will never tell you
"don't talk to strangers"

because we are each of us strangers
one to another
mysterious in our bodies,
the connections between us
ascending like separate stone wells
from the same dark waters
under the earth

But tonight you delight me like a lover
so that my thigh muscles twitch
and the nipples of my breasts
rise and remember
your small mouth
until I am laughing to the marrow of my bones
and I want to shout
Bless you, my daughter, bless you, bless you;
I have created the world in thirteen years
and it is good.

—Penelope Scambly Schott, Portland, OR

171

Penelope Schott is a former poetry professor and the author of several books of poetry. She received the 2004 Turning Point Poetry Prize.

Peanut Butter and Chocolate Milk, 1959

I was twelve when I started running. I was the youngest in my class, and so while I was still playing with dolls, girls around me were already getting their period. I did not get mine till I was fourteen, and at that point I was desperate for it to happen. I was doing breast-enhancement exercises in front of the mirror and buying Kotex. I had heard that if you gained weight, that might accelerate the onset of a period. So to boost my caloric intake, I started eating peanut butter sandwiches and drinking chocolate milk before going to bed, and I gained about fifteen pounds. When my period came, I remember being so happy. I always loved having my period. It reminded me how life is a cycle, and how I was a creature of nature. I felt powerful because of it.

—Kathrine Switzer, New Zealand and New York, NY

In the mid-1960s, Kathrine Switzer broke the gender barrier in long-distance running as the first woman to officially complete the Boston Marathon. She won the New York City Marathon in 1974.

Tamora Pierce Saves the Day, 2006

I grew up in an aware Christian family, so I'd gotten *somewhat* of a sex talk—you know, the "sex is bad" kind of thing. But I had never gotten the period talk.

In my family, when you become a woman, you can get your ears pierced. So every year, new girls would show up with their ears pierced at family reunions, and we would all know why: "Oh, there's another one!" I didn't want to get my ears pierced because everyone would know and I really just didn't see the need. So I waited a year and got them pierced when my sister got hers.

I don't know what I would have done without Tamora Pierce. I was a really big fan and read all her books. The little sex ed I knew came from Alanna (heroine of The Song of the Lioness Quartet series). The books aren't negative at all about it; they celebrate it! It's natural and comes regularly, and I knew that if it was written about in such a widely read book, it wasn't something to be ashamed about. And I could use the books as a means of talking to my sisters about it. My brother read it, too, so he wasn't weirded out at all. That was really nice.

—Madeleine, New York, NY

Madeleine is a fifteen-year-old high school student. She has a twin brother who isn't grossed out by periods.

Editor's Note: For Madeleine, her brother, and Tamora Pierce fans everywhere, the next story is for you.

Slippery in the Stairwell, 1965

Unlike a lot of girls at that time, I knew quite a bit about what to expect. My mother, who had studied nursing for two years, had been careful to explain the Facts of Life in a way I could understand from the time I was very young. Around about fifth grade, I discovered I could put off bedtime if I asked her to explain to me about the uterus and the ovaries again. (She drew pictures, which was time-consuming for her and more stay-up time for me.) I was a problem child for the poor teacher who was given the job of (highly controversial and new) sex education for girls, because I would show off my learning and use the scientific terms when I asked questions. (Okay, I admit it, I was a geek as a kid.)

I spent fifth and most of sixth grade in a state of high excitement, waiting and hoping for that first period, the sign that I was a woman at last. I knew it would be soon, because when I bounced and watched myself in the mirror, I began to see jiggling, which was my mother's bottom-line requirement for a first bra. Until the boys in my sixth-grade class noted it, I hadn't realized I was getting hair under my arms—another milestone. So I waited, even though it seemed like I waited *forever*.

I can still see the time and place where I got that first hint. In the hall outside our sixth-grade classroom, as I was walking down the stairs, I felt some kind of slipperiness between the cheeks of my rear. It never occurred to me to look until I was home. My parents were out, we had a babysitter, and I startled her immensely by joyfully screaming, "I've got my period! I've got my period!" She celebrated with me, having reached that longed-for state two years before me. The first thing I did was find the pads and the little belt (in those days, you either hung a pad off a little belt inside your underwear or you pinned it to your underwear—no stick-on napkins then), assemble them as my mother had shown me, and put my first napkin on. When my parents came home, I got hugs and congratulations.

By the next day, I was introduced to the downside of having a period: my first, very mild case of cramps as my parents wondered if I should go to a roller-skating party. In later months, I would learn about worse cramps, lower back pain, and the fact that you can't wear a napkin to a swimming party, which included a painful first introduction to a tampon. But I have never forgotten those first few hours, the slippery feeling that led to triumph, that feeling that I'd passed the last test of womanhood and could conquer the world.

—Tamora Pierce, New York

Tamora is the author of the best-selling teen fantasy series The Song of the Lioness Quartet.

175

Down Under, 1983

My period arrived when I was about thirteen and in the first year of high school. I knew what was going on; that was inevitable at my school, an all-girl private Catholic school, where all aspects of sex education were covered and covered again in a gradual and subversive five-year strategy to turn us off to sex before marriage.

My reaction to my first period was one of great sadness. I think I woke to that sticky feeling and rushed to the bathroom to investigate. Whatever time of day it was, I do remember emerging from the bathroom in quite a state, running to my bedroom and throwing myself on the bed, teary-eyed. I was particularly close to my dad, and I felt grief-stricken at the thought that I would no longer be his special buddy. . . . Would he still want me to mow the lawns?

(Yes!)

By period #2 I was in denial. I was due to spend a long weekend with a boarder from my school on a farm in the midst of Western Australia's wheat belt. Trips to my friend's farm were outdoor, tomboy affairs—riding horses and motorbikes, driving farm vehicles, rabbit shooting, hanging out with my friend's dad and brother doing farm stuff. Loaded up with a bag of pads, I was determined to do all the usual fun things and keep my secret to myself. Unfortunately, my mum had called ahead to my friend's mother, letting her know of my "state." When I arrived, within earshot of my friend's father and brother, I was given a lecture on "pad protocol" on the farm. The soiled items were to be wrapped in newspaper and carried out to the forty-four-gallon drum that served as a household incinerator in the backyard. There was to be no hiding and no denial. Every time I took a parcel out to the drum, I felt like the eyes of all the men were following me.

It seems I got over the trauma. My sister tells me that it was me, lil' sis, who taught her all about tampons. No more pads or, as she put it, no more riding around on a cotton-wool saddle. And the seeds of my commercial instincts were sown—apparently I asked for an increase in pocket money to cover any emergencies.

—Jenni Deslandes, Sydney, Australia

Jenni is a former McKinsey consultant.

Time for Prayer, 2006

Before my first period, I always looked upon the event as leading directly to womanhood, a sort of immediate dawning of maturity. When it finally came, far earlier than I wanted or expected, it was none of the above. It was actually just sort of sticky.

I was eleven years old, and a dark substance was pouring out of me and staining my underwear. Being rather reserved about private matters, just like the rest of my family, I was not fully prepared to run into the streets and scream out, "I have blood gushing out of my vagina!"

Instead, I waited. It was two whole days of toilet-paper padding before I cornered my mother, far away from my brothers and father, and hissed out, "I think I had my period." Her reaction was far from what I expected—she was ecstatic. She grabbed hold of me in a display of more affection than I had seen in quite a while (not that she isn't affectionate or a wonderful mother). Rather than explaining pads, possible symptoms, and answering any period questions, my mother told me that I had to pray five times a day. As a Muslim, there are special rituals that occur after the beginning of menstruation and during each cycle. As the official onset of womanhood, it is required that some activities be completed daily, such as regular prayers. However, women may not pray during the menstrual cycle, and afterward there is a special way of bathing and shaving.

None of this was what I wanted to hear after notifying

my mother of my state. I just wanted to know how to make the blood stop. When her excitement wore off, my mom got around to explaining the basics—clean stained clothes immediately, no flushing of pads, and get used to this happening every month. She then relayed the news to every female member of my extended family. Privacy? Not a chance.

—Fatema Maswood, Cromwell, CT

Fatema Maswood is a high school student who does theater and has an affinity for outdoor music festivals.

The Right Place at the Right Time, 1952

I remember getting my first period vividly. I was living in Carmel Valley with my mother, since my parents were living apart after a bitter and contentious divorce followed by tension-filled visits by my stepmother and my father, whom I adored and did not see very frequently. It so happened that my father was on one of his infrequent, tension-filled visits when I got my first period. In the midst of all the confusion, discomfort, and looking for and applying various ungainly things—(not tampons, which I found out about only years later)—things that I had not been introduced to, I remember my father saying, "I am glad that I was here." I was completely mystified as to why he would say that, since the entire episode was a source of discomfort, misery, and embarrassment to me. But later, I did understand that comment, and appreciated it.

—Leigh Bienen, Evanston, IL

Leigh Bienen is a writer, a lawyer, and a teacher. Her fiction can be found in The Left-Handed Marriage. *She is the director of the Chicago Historical Homicide Project (http://homicide.northwestern.edu) and the Florence Kelley Project (http://FlorenceKelley.norwestern.edu).*

Blood Month, 1979

The world doesn't stop when someone dies. You want it to. You damned well pray it will. But it doesn't. It just keeps going. Unthinkingly. The moon still turns in the sky, the sun still rises, the air still moves in and out of your lungs, the blood in and out of your capillaries. Your body breathes and builds. Despite you.

If I could have told my body to stop when my sister died, I would have. I would have folded it up like an old gray T-shirt and stuffed it in the back of the closet. Left it there for five years. At least five years, because it takes longer than that to heal. But five years' respite would have been better than five minutes. Only bodies aren't like that. They're like the sun and the wind. Like fields of red soil and the rain. At once strange and familiar. We can pattern their cycles, but we can't control them. They're moon-governed. Stir-crazy.

So, here we are. It's November. "Blood Month," according to the Reverend Mr. Bede, historian of old, on account of all the animals that got slaughtered by owners who didn't think they'd make it through the winter. I'm probably on the list—my head hurts, my heart aches, and I'm feeling, well, weak at the knees.

My sister's bedroom is full of toys. Her clothes are hanging in the airing cupboard. I dig past a pile of her underwear each time I reach for my own. No one speaks. No one knows what to say, let alone what to do.

Unsure myself, I sieve what I am told for meaning. Mine information for a nugget of gold, a hint of truth, a sense of what has happened. I become an expert at decoding things half-said: cancer, white blood, God. And I try to understand Blood Month.

The emptiness of the house is overbearing. I get out of it as soon as possible, even if it is only to go back to school. Once there, I don't know what to do with myself. I'm not prepared for the sideways looks or the indifference. When the teachers talk to me, I clam up. The kids don't try. Except one.

"Yer sister skiving again?"

"Er, no."

"Haven't seen her for weeks."

"No."

"Where is she, then?"

"Dead."

"You're joking!"

After that I don't respond so clearly. Don't say what I think. Half the time I don't even know what I think. I'm hiding out in that small space between the edge of my self and my shadow. All I know is that they don't teach you about things like death at school.

They don't teach you about bodies either, not properly. They do the science bit—the anatomy, the eggs, mating and all. But they don't talk about "body-mindedness"— when the mind is full of things the body should do but can't, like produce good blood cells.

And I've never heard them speak of "body-bloody-mindedness"—when the body does its own thing, regardless of the consequences, like produce white blood cells that refuse to mature; even if immature, they fail to function.

And they certainly don't spend much time on "body-bloodiness." Well, they should, because the body is full of blood. Five and a half million cubic millimeters of it, to be precise. That's eight pints in the average woman. Eleven and a half cans of cola.

And it's not just the quantity that's impressive—it's all that living and dying in one small space. Blood cells only live four months. They're born in our bones, disintegrate in our veins or get rounded up to be destroyed in our liver or spleen. It's a closed system, like an experiment. Blood is trapped in our bodies and branded with a sell-by date, unless it escapes from the womb.

Blood Month. My first period, of course, and I'm not prepared. My body doesn't understand the cycle of bloodletting any better than I do. Starts with a dribble, ends with a rush—a gush of blood down my legs. I dab at it with the bleached white toilet paper our school insists on stocking. The blood soaks in—brightly screaming, "I'm here and will be here every month, if you're lucky. Every three weeks or six weeks, or even bimonthly, if you're not. And I won't come alone. I'll come on waves of hysteria, on bloated limbs, or aching breasts, and if you're paying one iota of attention, you'll know I'm on my way long before I arrive."

Obviously I haven't been paying any attention at all. I'm saved from lifelong humiliation by a girl I hardly know but who knows enough about girls getting their first periods to know they rarely have what they need when it happens. She ushers me into the school bathroom. Orders me to rub at the spot of blood on my uniform with soap, and leaves me locked in a stall, a thick pad in my hand and the word "curse" banging in my brain like a slammed door.

Blood Month. How could I have not known this was about to happen? I'd been assuming that my swollen breasts were grief, my bloated belly—grief, and grief, my inarticulate tongue. I should have known better—in life, you should assume nothing. Our cycles are not set in stone: your body might not work tomorrow, your blood might not carry oxygen to the heart, your heart may not even beat. But then again, it might.

Blood Month. One day I wake up and my sister's body is a delicate shade of blue. What's left of her blood has drained from her face, leaving it with the pallor of a frying pan.

One day I get up and my body starts bleeding. But I'm not sick or dying. In fact, I've never been more alive. I'm fertile.

The symptomatology of blood is far from simple.

I hide my new status like a secret. Slip it in a velvet purse and bury it in my heart. I don't want anyone to know that I have life for two when she didn't have enough life for herself.

After school I visit the supermarket. I search the wall of sanitary products for something resembling the pad I'm using. The choice is overwhelming: different colors, sizes, shapes. Finally I pick a dark green box because I like the color and the serious young face that stares out from it. She feels like a sister. Seems to know how I feel.

I walk up to the checkout casually. I want the gum-chewing cashier to think I've been doing this all my life, been being a woman, just like her.

"Crack!" goes the gum.

"Tring!" goes the till.

"Two-fifty," the voice.

She hands me my box in a red plastic bag. So much for velvet secrets.

The Reverend Mr. Bede wouldn't have known the term "adolescent." They didn't have them in his day. There were adults and children. Women or girls. Teenagers didn't exist, nor did teenage angst. So why am I feeling funny about a bit of blood? The fact that my body has blood to spill while my sister's didn't have enough to keep it going? The fact that I'm a woman now, and the long and short of it is that I'm marriageable, bedable, impregnable? I can't help hoping that this is only the first stage of the cycle. That something more important, more meaningful, happens later.

Blood Month. First blood, it tips the world sideways like a first death or a first kiss, sends you with very little control toward something new and inevitable, like Mr. Bede's sharp blades.

There'll be blood now, every month. The sight of it never failing to shock. The scent of it, too, as if it's been designed to impress with a mixture of horror and awe, the life force it contains. As if that unforgiving smell, that breathing color is only there to remind you that blood equals life. And that life is a paradox—a liquid fire: burning up memories and dreams, pooling genes and emotion.

First blood. Some offer it to their ancestors, to honor the family bloodline. Others offer it to the earth, to honor the land they live and take from. Some throw coming-of-age parties, others celebrate quietly with the women of their family, telling stories and laughing.

There is not much laughter in my house right now. No celebration either.

But it's Blood Month all right, and the nights draw in early. On my way home, I cut through the park, passing the cotton tree I used to climb with my sister. As I approach, her laughter ghosts through me. I stop. Steady myself by holding the tree's silver trunk. I don't want to cry here. I crouch down instead, concentrating on spreading my hands flat on the grass and feeling every blade that touches them. Under my hands is a tangle of tree roots and, not far away, my sister's body lying stiller than stone, bluer than the blood of any queen. I close my eyes, curl up at the base of the tree, and hug my red bag to my heart. There goes my celebration.

When I open my eyes, I see the tip of a dark green box pointing up at the moon in the sky. I pull my new friend out of the plastic bag so she can see it too. She looks cold in the half-light, worried. She doesn't know how easy her flat existence is. She needs to move on. To grow up a little.

I rip open the box and empty out the pads. Then, very carefully, I tear the girl away from her green world. I'm going to introduce her to a new one—a garden of grass and trees, with wind and rain, and the moon ever moving through the sky. I'm going to show her what it feels like to be made new. To have unknown hands push a "start" button in your body without giving any warning. We're going to walk from the simple worlds we have known, together.

We'll mark the moving on in our lives with a shrine. I set up her image on a mound of earth and pile stones on either side of it. It's as if I'm trying to bury the life she is walking from. Bury my own at the same time. As if I'm trying to tell her that though she thinks she has lost everything, she is being reborn. That each of the stones I add to her shrine is a blessing, for with each different-shaped stone, she will have good grounding. Will know that nothing is ever the same. Nothing is fixed. The womb wall thickens and thins. Day becomes night, and night becomes light. The moon shifts from new to full and waning. There is no lull between the stages, no waiting for us to catch our breath. The tide changes, and we must flow with it or be beached. There can be no still point in between for explanation, preparation, or pause.

"Blood Month," I whisper. Mr. Bede sharpening his blades in the shortening days, his back to the chill of winter.

"Blood Moon," she replies, her eyes on the sky. Mr. Bede's sharp blades and his big bald head are mirrors for her beauty.

The moon isn't governed by butchers' blades or months when blood once flowed. For every Blood Month there are thirteen Blood Moons. Thirteen bloody cycles—because one isn't enough to understand the enormity of what we are and what we may become. Because one isn't enough for all the waxing and waning in our bodies, all the changing in our lives.

Blood Month. Blood Moon. Blood Womb.

The body breathing and building, despite you.

—Sandra Guy, Paris, France

Sandra is a British writer living in Paris. Her writing has appeared in literary journals in France, Britain, and the United States. She is currently at work on a fantasy novel for teenagers based on the winter solstice.

Late Bloomer, 1998

It didn't come until I was a senior in high school. And, even then, it wasn't the way it was supposed to. The doctor gave me these little green pills. "Progesterone. To kick your body into gear." I was, to say the least, a late bloomer.

Nevertheless, I had been fully prepared by sixth grade, thanks to awkward educational-film screenings at my elementary school during which the grown-ups separated the boys and girls. What did they think would happen if we stayed together? Why shouldn't boys know about menstroo-ation?

In elementary school, I pored over Judy Blume's *Are You There God? It's Me, Margaret*. Margaret and her friends had a secret stash of "sanitary napkins," just in case. They practiced, too, and recited "I must, I must, I must increase my bust!" with fervor and dedication. When would it come for me? Maybe when the dreamy boy across the street practiced his trombone? Or perhaps over a bowl of mac 'n' cheese? I wanted so badly to be admitted into that club of girls who'd had it.

Periods, not to mention breasts or boyfriends, remained a mystery long after junior high. But the thing is, I had armpit hair in sixth grade, way before my girlfriends.

While I longed for rosy pips of breasts, instead I got razor burn and ingrown hairs from my pink plastic Bic disposable razor.

Eventually I settled complacently into my late-bloomer identity. No boyfriend. No kissing. No need for a bra. So at age sixteen-almost-seventeen, when I found the brown stuff in my undies, it was kind of anticlimactic. I expected trumpets, fanfare, a red carpet. But it wasn't even red. It was brown guck. Stale. Long overdue.

—Emily Hagenmaier, Los Angeles, CA

Emily is a social worker.

History Sometimes Repeats Itself, 1970

188

I was ten at the time, and it was summertime. My entire family (four sisters and a brother) was gathered in the living room at our stone summer house in Gaithersburg, Maryland. The sky darkened, and it began to hail golf-ball-sized chunks of ice. I am not making this up. The windows started breaking. We couldn't believe this was happening because it was July. Needless to say, I was not the center of attention, and I believe I waited until the following morning to make my announcement. My older sister was very disgusted that I got there before she did.

I remember being somewhat prepared for the blood because my school had herded the girls into the girls' bathroom for a talk about menstruation earlier in the year. What always nauseated me, however, were those big, bulging Kotex pads drenched in blood. Tampons just seem so much more civilized and probably would have worked just fine at the time.

My story doesn't end there, however. Two years later, my period stopped suddenly. I was given estrogen and progesterone pills to self-administer. When I took the medication, I accidentally mixed the order up and bled continuously for two weeks. Finally, I told my mom, who took one look at me and rushed me to the hospital. I was hemorrhaging. Oddly enough, a year earlier, she had hemorrhaged after her sixth pregnancy and almost died. I remember being home from school that day as my dad helped her down the stairs and into the car. After she left, I walked into her bathroom. It was filled with big, white towels seeped in blood. History sometimes repeats itself.

—Marianne Bernstein, Philadelphia, PA

One of six children, Marianne is a photographer, filmmaker, teacher, and arts activist and is the mother of two sons.

Twelve-Step Program, 1946

Most people today are familiar with twelve-step programs for addiction. Back in 1946, I had my very own twelve-step program for puberty.

There were exactly twelve wooden steps from my grandmother Bubbie K's front porch to the sidewalk. Those were the twelve steps that I took as I left her home one sunny

Sunday afternoon. After I kissed my Bubbie K good-bye, I walked down those steps to my parents waiting at the sidewalk. A large drop of blood appeared on each step as I descended. I can still see my mother and father standing frozen and speechless.

The three of us were dumbfounded. But my Bubbie K came to the rescue. She had been on the front porch, waiting to wave good-bye and throw kisses, as was her custom. She ran to me, cupped my face in her hands, and said, "Mazel tov, now you can make babies!"

I shall never forget her words. Not only did they save the day, but they were also loving and positive. She put her arms around me, and we walked into the house so that she could give me something to take care of me until I got home. Then she proudly walked me down those twelve steps and presented me as a woman to my parents.

Not a word was spoken on the way home. On my next weekly visit to my Bubbie K, she told me how to make babies. I don't remember exactly what she said, but I know she said that it was fun. That was not the message I got from my parents when they gave me the traditional anatomical lecture years later.

—Marcia Nalebuff, Newton, MA

Marcia is an exacting copy editor and a volunteer for Boston Aid to the Blind. She enjoys spoiling her grandchildren.

Flow, 1983

I thought that I got my period when I was twelve.

I longed for the big day like a bridezilla after scoring an engagement ring. I would play dress-up, trying on my mom's belted maxi pads like some girls try on jewelry and makeup. No floppy hats and faux pearls for me; it was clumpy cotton all the way. Being a woman seemed to carry so many advantages: receiving expensive jewelry on special occasions, having a far superior shoe selection, getting rescued out of burning buildings first, and being visited by your "friend," a monthly reminder that you are, indeed, a woman. I could not wait.

You can imagine my excitement when I woke up one summer morning at the age of twelve and saw it. It was red, perfect, and round, looking back at me, sitting silently on my white Hanes panties. There was no announcement, no fanfare, none of that—just a little spot that was, I thought, the beginning of my adult life. I would now be understood, regarded, counted. The only other girl who had her period in my class was the most popular girl in school, a girl I hung around with, though I was maybe only her third-best friend. This would bump me up for sure. We could talk about which tampons were best and commiserate about cramps, bloating, and all that stuff. I couldn't wait to drone, "I have my period," as if I were a lifer.

But even as, one by one, all of my friends starting getting their periods that year, mine disappeared. It came and went before I ever even had time to hate it. Months passed since that first sighting and still . . . nothing. Not even a drop. Maybe I hadn't really had my period after all. Maybe it was some hormone- and peer pressure–driven delusion I had suffered in my rush toward womanhood—a case of wishful spotting. In my more rational moments, I convinced myself I'd probably just nicked myself shaving my upper thigh and gotten some blood on my underwear when I put them on.

Whatever the truth might have been, I was still prepubescent and ashamed. I kept it to myself, fearful of what rung on the social ladder I would slip down to in my friends' eyes. "The monkey has a bloody nose, I'm just going to stay home tonight," one of my friends would say, politely declining a sleepover invite. "I don't feel like swimming, I'm at the movies," another would yell to one across the room. I was trapped in an endless series of quippy menses euphemisms. I joined in. I got the joke, but I wasn't laughing. How could it be that I was riding so high on the cotton pony, and now nothing? I wanted to be at the movies, too.

I kept up the period lie for months, traumatizing myself, afraid I'd be found out for the fraud I was, until one fateful day—my thirteenth birthday party at the Rostraver ice-skating rink. All my friends were there. I felt horrible and kept running to the bathroom because I had such bad stomach cramps. Then, after I don't know how many trips to the toilet, I saw it. A red spot. There it was again! Was it mocking me? Was it for real? Here to stay or just another false positive? I knew one thing—that I couldn't trust it.

I ran out and whispered the news to my mom, who was the only person on the planet who knew the real truth and loved me anyway, looking for an objective opinion and a little reassurance. Suddenly I felt a little gush. I was expecting to feel resentful, like, so nice of you to show up, or maybe totally over it, like when you see those faded, brittle Christmas wreaths still hanging on your neighbor's door in August. Instead, I felt afraid and exhilarated at the same time. Houston, we have flow!

My mother went out to the lobby and got me one of those vending-machine maxi pads. It was huge. I'm sure it could be seen right through my pants. Normally, that would be humiliating to a woman, but not me; I wanted everyone to see my clump. It was something I'd wanted for so long, something I appreciated, something that I was proud of. In fact, if there were a "My daughter got her period at Rostraver skating rink" bumper sticker, I would have seriously considered slapping it on my mom's white Chevy Citation. I lay on the bench, where everyone had their shoes after changing into skates, and held my stomach. I could do that now for real. I did have cramps. I was no longer living a lie. I was free.

—Tonya Hurley, New York, NY

Tonya is an indie film writer and director as well as the author of the novel ghostgirl. *She has produced two hit TV series and is the creator of Mary-Kate and Ashley brand video games.*

You Always Remember Your First

I remember my first period very well; what I don't remember is my last.

—Carla Cohen, Washington, DC

Carla Cohen is a writer and the owner of an independent bookstore, Politics and Prose.

Euphemisms and Code Words

Arts and crafts week at panty camp
At the movies
Aunt Flo
Aunt Tillie from Red Bank
Being unwell
Big red
Cleanup in aisle one
Closed for maintenance
Congratulations! It's an egg!
The curse
Drip drop
Falling off the roof
Full stop
Getting my friend
Having the painters in
Hemorrhaging
In my moon
It
The leak
Miss Dot

The monkey has a bloody nose
The monthlies
Monthly bill
Murder scene
My cherry is in sherry
My communist friend
My friend's visiting
My punctuation
On the rag
Ordering l'omelette rouge
Raining down south

Rebooting the ovarian operating system
The redcoats have landed
Riding the cotton pony
Riding the red wave
That time of the month
Untimely moment

Learn More

BOOKS

ANTHROPOLOGY

Blood Magic: The Anthropology of Menstruation, Thomas Buckley and Alma Gottlieb, eds. Berkeley: University of California Press, 1988.

The Curse: Confronting the Last Unmentionable Taboo: Menstruation by Karen Houppert. New York: Farrar, Strauss and Giroux, 1999.

The Curse: A Cultural History of Menstruation by Janice Delaney, Mary Jane Lupton, and Emily Toth. Champaign, IL: University of Illinois Press, 1988.

FICTION

Are You There God? It's Me, Margaret by Judy Blume. New York: Bradbury Press, 1970.

The Red Tent by Anita Diamant. New York: Picador, 1997.

HEALTH RESOURCES

The Care & Keeping of You: The Body Book for Girls by Valorie Lee Schaefer. Middleton, WI: Pleasant Company Publications, 1998.

Growing Up: It's a Girl Thing: Straight Talk about First Bras, First Periods, and Your Changing Body by Mavis Jukes. New York: Alfred A. Knopf, 1998.

Our Bodies, Ourselves: A New Edition for a New Era by Judy Norsigian and the Boston Women's Health Book Collective. New York: Touchstone, 2005.

The Period Book: Everything You Don't Want to Ask (But Need to Know) by Karen Gravelle. New York: Walker Books for Young Readers, 2006.

WEB SITES

www.beinggirl.com: a site where girls can track their periods, ask questions, and share funny stories.

www.mum.org: an online museum of menstruation, with historical resources, an ad archive, and a great selection of jokes.

www.tamponcase.com: a company with a good sense of humor that sells cool tampon cases.

MOVIES AND VIDEOS (FOR A LAUGH)

The Period Dance: the best Tampax ad out there. Available on YouTube at www.youtube.com/watch?v=r-4APMv2QKo. *Superbad* (the dance scene): periods and dirty dancing don't always mix.

Do More

In Kenya, the Health and Water Foundation provides water, private toilets, and sanitary supplies to rural schools in order to keep girls in school. Girls with no sanitary supplies stay home, and even those who do have supplies often choose to stay at home in order to avoid the lack of privacy at exposed outdoor toilets. A further problem for girls is that many schools lack even a single female teacher or counselor. The royalties from this book will support the foundation's School Water and Sanitation Project, which provides sanitary supplies and private toilets. Started in 2007, this project has already helped hundreds of girls in the Nyamira District and ensures that each school has at least one female teacher to serve as a sex-education counselor for girls. Learn more at www.healthandwater.org.

Other organizations with similar missions in Africa include the Campaign for Female Education (www.camfed.org), CARE (Basic and Girls' Education Unit, www.care.org), Forum for African Women Educationalists (FAWE; www.fave.org), Save the Children's program in Ethiopia (www.savethechildren.org), and UNICEF (www.unicef.org).

In Zimbabwe, two interesting efforts working directly to provide sanitary supplies are the Girl Child Network (www.gcn.org.zw) and ACT-Southern Africa, via its Dignity! Period. campaign (www.actsa.org).

In India, Seva Mandir works to alleviate poverty through its many environmental, educational, and health programs. Funds from this book will be donated to support its women's empowerment and health education programs in Udaipur. Through its grassroots outreach, Seva Mandir has affected the lives of more than ten thousand women in the area, and now it will reach even more. Learn more at www.sevamandir.org.

Girls Inc. is a youth organization that promotes girls' empowerment through extracurricular educational programs. It is one of the most established organizations of this type and has more than fifty affiliates across the United States. Funds from this book will support its most popular program, which teaches girls to see beyond gender stereotypes and learn how to take responsibility for their own bodies. The program teaches personal sexual health and provides a safety network for open discussions as well as access to health care. Learn more at www.girlsinc.org.

Planned Parenthood is the largest provider of sexual education and health services in the United States. It is one of the few organizations that provide accurate medical education to teens, men, and women about safe-sex practices, STDs, and reproductive health-care options. Funds from this book will support its involvement in public health policy that helps keep health-care centers, sexual education, and contraception affordable and accessible. Learn more at www.plannedparenthood.org.

Choice USA is a youth-led organization that seeks to protect women's reproductive rights. Providing college campuses across the states with educational workshops and publicized by respected young leaders, Choice USA is one of the freshest voices in today's women's health movement. Funds from this book will support its Reproductive Justice Organizing Academy, which provides classes, informational sessions, and training to help young women mobilize communities to promote reproductive health and freedom. Learn more at www.choiceusa.org.

Acknowledgments

While it is possible for a girl to go through her first period on her own, there is no way to put together a book about first periods without a lot of people's help. I first want to thank all the women who shared their stories. They are the greatest risk takers here, and it is their words that bring these pages to life. Many stepped out of their comfort zones and revealed, often for the first time, what had happened during their first period. I especially want to thank the early contributors, who graciously gave me their stories when this was just a high school project.

Without Barbara Monteiro, this would still be a high school project. She opened the door to the publishing world, leading me to Victoria Skurnick, who in turn directed me to the perfect agent. As a first-time writer, I owe the world to the wonderful Susan Ginsburg for giving me a chance. Her faith in the project was contagious and led me to Jonathan Karp, who has been a dream of an editor. Between the two of them, I could not have asked for more enthusiastic and generous mentors. Bethany Strout and Colin Shepherd, who work with Susan and Jonathan, respectively, expertly worked behind the scenes to make everything go swimmingly.

I owe special thanks to several other women who helped behind the scenes, making sure the call for stories was distributed far and wide. Lisa Siciliano brought in a veritable cornucopia of stories, including one from her grandmother! Katie Pichotta served as the greatest indexer, fact-checker, hunter-gatherer, and sounding board that anyone could wish for. Marianne Bernstein both shared her story and took a most flattering picture of me for the book flap (not an easy task, considering I was in the middle of finals). Kristen Azzara provided deft and elegant copyediting. Thanks also to Patty Boyd, Angie Hurlbut, and Leslie Kuo for their early editorial and design help.

Many people read early versions of the manuscript, gave fresh-eyed feedback, and helped connect me to women with stories to tell: Elizabeth Alexander, Deborah Berman, Fran Brent, Roxanne Coady, Claire Connors, Deb Fleischman, Deb Margolin, Lori Gottlieb, Barbra Hendra, Moira Kelly, Maureen Kelly, Betty Monz, Marcia Nalebuff, Helen Rees, Barbara Rifkind, Takudzwa Shumba, Janet Siroto, Jeffrey Sonnenfeld (a guy!), Whitney Sparks, and Cheryl Weisenfeld. My teachers at Choate Rosemary Hall supported me through my senior research project on menarche: Ms. Biddiscombe and Ms. Nesslage, thank you! Thank you, too, classmates at Choate, for your cheers during my schoolwide assembly speech about first periods. Once I saw that freshman boys could take a speech about periods open-mindedly, I knew there was hope for this book.

I am indebted to Eve Ensler and in awe of the bravery it took for her to create *The Vagina Monologues*, the play that paved the way for this collection of menstruation monologues. I am similarly grateful to Gloria Steinem, whose hilarious and provocative essay "If Men Could Menstruate" first taught me to see periods with a sense of humor and as something worth proclaiming.

Last, the two people to whom I owe my greatest thanks are my parents, Helen Kauder and Barry Nalebuff. My mother's guiding hand shepherded me through the entire process. This book sowed the seeds for a new and wonderful stage in our mother-daughter relationship. My dad impressed me by being more comfortable talking about periods than I am. He has been cheering me on from the sidelines since day one and is my biggest fan. Without them and their unwavering support, this book would not be in your hands.

Permissions

"The Wrath of the Gods" (page 86) copyright © 2001 by Jill Bialosky, from *Subterranean: Poems by Jill Bialosky*. Used by permission of Alfred A. Knopf, a division of Random House, Inc.

"Locked in a Room with Dosai" (page 88) copyright © 2002 by Shobha Sharma, from *Kitchen Stories* by Shobha Sharma (Jane's Stories Press Foundation). Used by permission of the author.

"Letters" (page 99) from *Connecting the Dots* by Maxine Kumin. Copyright © 1996 by Maxine Kumin. Excerpted by permission of W. W. Norton & Company, Inc.

Cover art from the 1928 Australian edition of *Marjorie May's Twelfth Birthday* (page 100) is used by permission of the Curator of Heath and Medicine at the Powerhouse Museum, Sydney, Australia.

The advertisement "Unwanted Attention" (page 103) is used by permission of Leo Burnett USA and Tampax.

"If Men Could Menstruate" (page 114) updated version copyright © 1978 by Gloria Steinem. Used by permission of the author.

"Progressive Parenting" (page 156) copyright © 2001 by Nancy Gruver and Joe Kelly. Excerpted by permission of the authors.

Subject Index

The African American Experience
    Loss and Gain of Responsibility (1969), 40
    Memory: Day 1 (1973), 144

All Alone
    Euro Disney (1992), 161
    I Know You Are Not There, God. It's Me, Kate (1990), 66
    The Lie (1948), 20
    My Second First Period (1977), 139
    My Support System Was a Box (1977), 101

Alternative Uses
    Blood on the Tracks (1972), 58
    Mattress Pad (1990), 80

Belt, Napkin, and Tampon Incidents
    Going to X-tremes (1982), 25
    Hot Dog on a String (1993), 51
    A Jealous Vajayjay (1981), 34

Bittersweet Stories
    Desperately Delayed (1970), 76
    Germany (1942), 21
    The Harness (1961), 149
    History Sometimes Repeats Itself (1970), 188
    Let Down (2007), 75
    The Ming Period (1999), 43
    My Second First Period (1977), 139

(Bittersweet Stories, continued)
Out of the Closet (1968), 119
Step Toward Womanhood, but with Stepmom (1983), 106

Brothers and Dads
The Blusher (2002), 49
Desperately Delayed (1970), 76
Down Under (1983), 175
Euro Disney (1992), 161
Glamorous, but Not for Long (1981), 64
Ink Blots and Milk Spots (1987), 59
A Jealous Vajayjay (1981), 34
Loss and Gain of Responsibility (1969), 40
Memory: Day 1 (1973), 144
Oh, Brother (1993), 13
The Right Place at the Right Time (1952), 178
Showdown at the HoJo (1968), 159
Tsihabuhkai (1962), 129
Yodelay Uh-Oh (1982), 108

Caught Between Two Cultures
Mehn-su (1992), 31
Time for Prayer (2006), 177

Celebrations
Cranberry Sauce (1993), 127
The Dream (1994), 132
If Men Could Menstruate, 114
The Simple Vase: Parts I and II (1997), 71, 74
Tamora Pierce Saves the Day (2006), 172

Disposal Challenges
Burning Secret (1966), 15
Down Under (1983), 175
Into the Woods (1964), 38
Out of the Closet (1968), 119
Proper Disposal (1993), 79

Dreams
The Dream (1994), 132

Early Starts

Barbies and Biology (1996), 97

A Coup at the Napkin Dispenser (1960), 145

History Sometimes Repeats Itself (1970), 188

Mehn-su (1992), 31

Fainting

The Earache (1975), 155

Showdown at the HoJo (1968), 159

Fishing Stories

Jaws (2004), 102

Proper Disposal (1993), 79

Holidays and Vacations

Andy Roddick's Serve (2003), 45

Cranberry Sauce (1993), 127

Dying in the Land of Dionysus (1972), 104

Euro Disney (1992), 161

Fear of Fourteen (1991), 16

Into the Woods (1964), 38

Jaws (2004), 102

No Gushing for Me, Please (1979), 82

Staining the Citroën (1970), 125

The White Dress (1971), 111

In the Classroom

The Artist (1968), 23

Oh, the "Joy" of Menses! (1987), 46

The Ming Period (1999), 43

A Puddle (1991), 118

Slippery in the Stairwell (1965), 173

Up at the Chalkboard (1979), 112

International Stories

Barbies and Biology (1996), 97

Chairman Mao's Period (1967), 56

Crushed Leaves in Kenya (2006), 135

Dress Appropriately (1974), 153

(International Stories, continued)
    Guatemala: Advice from a Cheesemaker (1953), 30
    Locked in a Room with Dosai (1962), 88
    Mattress Pad (1990), 80
    Up at the Chalkboard (1979), 112

It's Unfair
    Chairman Mao's Period (1967), 56
    Dress Appropriately (1974), 153

I Was Dying
    Andy Roddick's Serve (2003), 45
    Burning Secret (1966), 15
    Dying in the Land of Dionysus (1972), 104
    History Sometimes Repeats Itself (1970), 188
    Jaws (2004), 102
    Too Wet (1994), 28
    Up at the Chalkboard (1979), 112
    Where's My Belt? (1979), 136

Jewish Stories
    Bloody Bat Mitzvah (2002), 24
    Can I Sit on His Lap? (1916), 96
    Fear of Fourteen (1991), 16
    Germany (1942), 21
    The Simple Vase: Parts I and II (1997), 71, 74
    The Slap (1972), 83
    Step Toward Womanhood, but with Stepmom (1983), 106
    Twelve-Step Program (1946), 189

Judy Blume
    Bloody Bat Mitzvah (2002), 24
    Glamorous, but Not for Long (1981), 64
    I Know You Are Not There, God. It's Me, Kate (1990), 66
    Late Bloomer (1998), 187
    Mehn-su (1992), 31
    Oh, the "Joy" of Menses! (1987), 46
    The Von Trapps and Me (1980), 149

Where's My Belt? (1979), 136
Yodelay Uh-Oh (1982), 108

Late Starts
Can I Just Skip This Period? (1971), 32
Desperately Delayed (1970), 76
A Jealous Vajayjay (1981), 34
Late Bloomer (1998), 187
The Lie (1948), 20
Not Getting It (1980), 165
Operation Menstruation! (1998), 133
Peanut Butter and Chocolate Milk (1959), 171

Latina Stories
Señorita (1980), 94

Misconceptions
Andy Roddick's Serve (2003), 45
Burning Secret (1966), 15
Cranberry Sauce (1993), 127
Dying in the Land of Dionysus (1972), 104
Good-bye, Green Thumb (1942), 14
Guatemala: Advice from a Cheesemaker (1953), 30
Hot Dog on a String (1993), 51
Oh, the "Joy" of Menses! (1987), 46
Operation Menstruation! (1998), 133
Time for Prayer (2006), 177
Too Wet (1994), 28

Muslim Stories
Time for Prayer (2006), 177

Native American Stories
Tsihabuhkai (1962), 129

Not Telling
Burning Secret (1966), 15
Euro Disney (1992), 161
I Know You Are Not There, God. It's Me, Kate (1990), 66
The Lie (1948), 20

213

(Not Telling, continued)

My Second First Period (1977), 139

Out of the Closet (1968), 119

Señorita (1980), 94

Step Toward Womanhood, but with Stepmom (1983), 106

Old Wives' Tales

Good-bye, Green Thumb (1942), 14

Guatemala: Advice from a Cheesemaker (1953), 30

Parent Stories

Fear of Fourteen (1991), 16

Progressive Parenting (1993), 156

Proper Disposal (1993), 79

Simple as Salt (1967 and 2008), 92

The Simple Vase: Part I (1997), 71

Poems

blood relative (1976), 27

An excerpt from "Letters," 99

Memory: Day 1 (1973), 144

When you phoned home from California to tell me
    it had started, 170

The Wrath of the Gods (1970), 86

Sports Stories

The Blusher (2002), 27

Downward Dog (2004), 147

No Longer in Little League (1993), 161

Peanut Butter and Chocolate Milk (1959), 171

The Stain

The Artist (1968), 23

A Puddle (1991), 118

Up at the Chalkboard (1979), 112

The White Dress (1971), 111

Teens Today

Andy Roddick's Serve (2003), 45

Bloody Bat Mitzvah (2002), 24

The Blusher (2002), 49
Crushed Leaves in Kenya (2006), 135
Downward Dog (2004), 147
Jaws (2004), 102
Let Down (2007), 75
LOL {.} (2005), 57
Tamora Pierce Saves the Day (2006), 172
Time for Prayer (2006), 177

Unusual Circumstances
Bloody Bat Mitzvah (2002), 24
Germany (1942), 21
An Invisible Period (1981), 46
Locked in a Room with Dosai (1962), 88

Unusual Customs
Ink Blots and Milk Spots (1987), 59
Locked in a Room with Dosai (1962), 88
On Horseback (1960s), 163
Rescued by a Refugee (1941), 85
The Slap (1972), 83
Tamora Pierce Saves the Day (2006), 172

Vintage Stories
Can I Sit on His Lap? (1916), 96
The Curse (1939), 69
Germany (1942), 21
Good-bye, Green Thumb (1942), 14
The Lie (1948), 20
Rescued by a Refugee (1941), 85
Silence (1930s), 34
Twelve-Step Program (1946), 189

Wishful Thinking and False Alarms
Flow (1983), 191
Glamorous, but Not for Long (1981), 64
Ink Blots and Milk Spots (1987), 59
The Lie (1948), 20
Not Getting It (1980), 165

(Wishful Thinking and False Alarms, continued)
    On Horseback (1960s), 163
    Señorita (1980), 94

YA Authors
    Meg Cabot, 136
    Tonya Hurley, 191
    Michele Jaffe, 25
    Erica Jong, 16
    Patty Marx, 32
    Joyce Maynard, 119
    Megan McCafferty, 46
    Jacquelyn Mitchard, 92
    Tamora Pierce, 172
    Rachel Vail, 165
    Cecily von Ziegesar, 108

Author Index

Abegunde, M. Eliza Hamilton   Memory: Day 1 (1973), 144
Altintas, Aysegul   Barbies and Biology (1996), 97
Arthur, Emilia   Up at the Chalkboard (1979), 112
Asselin, Judy Nicholson   Desperately Delayed (1970), 76

Bashian, Jen   Andy Roddick's Serve (2003), 45
Bassman, Nina   Germany (1942), 21
Baumgardner, Jennifer   Glamorous, but Not for Long
                               (1981), 64
Bentley, Nina   The Artist (1968), 23
Bernstein, Marianne   History Sometimes Repeats Itself
                               (1970), 188
Bialosky, Jill   The Wrath of the Gods (1970), 86
Bienen, Leigh   The Right Place at the Right Time
                               (1952), 178
Boyd, Patricia E.   Blood on the Tracks (1972), 58

Cabot, Meg   Where's My Belt? (1979), 136
Caruso, Nancy   A Jealous Vajayjay (1981), 34
Cohen, Carla   You Always Remember Your
                               First, 194
Conant, Catherine   Proper Disposal (1993), 79

Davis, Lisa Selin   Step Toward Womanhood, but with
                               Stepmom (1983), 106
Dean, Jennifer Asanin   Operation Menstruation! (1998), 133
Devine, Ellen   Hot Dog on a String (1993), 51

Deslandes, Jenni   Down Under (1983), 175
Dodds, Debby   The Von Trapps and Me (1980), 149

Firke, Marian   Downward Dog (2004), 147
Flori   Guatemala: Advice from a
                            Cheesemaker (1953), 30
Foster, Elli   The Blusher (2002), 49
Freundlich-Hall, Sondra   blood relative (1976), 27

Gang, Barclay Rachael   Cranberry Sauce (1993), 127
Garmisa, Bonnie   My Support System Was a Box
                            (1977), 101
Gerhard, Lola   The Curse (1939), 69
Gerhard, Sharon   Into the Woods (1964), 38
Gottchalk, Lily   Jaws (2004), 102
Greenberg, Linda   Showdown at the HoJo (1968), 159
Gruver, Nancy, and Joe Kelly   Progressive Parenting (1993), 156
Guy, Sandra   Blood Month (1979), 179

Hagenmaier, Emily   Late Bloomer (1998), 187
Hickman, Sara   The Mermaid (1974), 168
Hu, Mary   Dying in the Land of Dionysus
                            (1972), 104
Hurley, Tonya   Flow (1983), 191

Jaffe, Michele   Going to X-tremes (1982), 25
Johnson-Roehr, Catherine   Staining the Citroën (1970), 125
Jong, Erica   Fear of Fourteen (1991), 16

Kandel, Thelma   Good-bye, Green Thumb (1942), 14
Kauder Nalebuff, Zoe   LOL {.} (2005), 57
Kelly, Joe, and Nancy Gruver   Progressive Parenting (1993), 156
Kovacic, Kathi   The White Dress (1971), 111
Kumin, Maxine   An excerpt from "Letters," 99

Lainer, Ilene   The Slap (1972), 83
Lee, Amy H.   Mehn-su (1992), 31

Lewis, Zannette — Loss and Gain of Responsibility (1969), 40

Lindroth, Linda — A Coup at the Napkin Dispenser (1960), 145

Ma, Xiao Ling — Chairman Mao's Period (1967), 56

Madeleine — Tamora Pierce Saves the Day (2006), 172

Madsen, Krista — Ink Blots and Milk Spots (1987), 59

Marx, Patty — Can I Just Skip This Period? (1971), 32

Maswood, Fatema — Time for Prayer (2006), 177

Matos, Kica — Señorita (1980), 94

Maynard, Joyce — Out of the Closet (1968), 119

McCafferty, Megan — Oh, the "Joy" of Menses! (1987), 46

Mitchard, Jacquelyn — Simple as Salt (1967 and 2008), 92

Moghaddam, Bita — Dress Appropriately (1974), 153

Murphy, Bernadette — My Second First Period (1977), 139

Mweu, Thatcher — Crushed Leaves in Kenya (2006), 135

Nalebuff, Marcia — Twelve-Step Program (1946), 189

Nelson, Miriam — The Earache (1975), 155

Pahdopony, Juanita — Tsihabuhkai (1962), 129

Pierce, Tamora — Slippery in the Stairwell (1965), 173

Rafia — Too Wet (1994), 28

Ray, Moira Kathleen — No Longer in Little League (1993), 161

Robbins, Deo — The Harness (1961), 149

Rosen, Sarah — Bloody Bat Mitzvah (2002), 24

S. — An Invisible Period (1981), 46

Schott, Penelope Scambly — When you phoned home from California to tell me it had started, 170

Schuster, Jessy	Euro Disney (1992), 161
Selinsky, Pearl Stein	Rescued by a Refugee (1941), 85
Sharma, Shobha	Locked in a Room with Dosai (1962), 88
Sherman, Annie	The Dream (1994), 132
Shutan, Suzan	Burning Secret (1966), 15
Shvarts, Aliza	The Ming Period (1999), 43
Siciliano, Elizabeth	Silence (1930s), 34
Steinem, Gloria	If Men Could Menstruate, 114
Story, Louise	Oh, Brother (1993), 13
Switzer, Kathrine	Peanut Butter and Chocolate Milk (1959), 171
Travers, Tatum	Let Down (2007), 75
Vail, Rachel	Not Getting It (1980), 165
Victor, Shalom	The Lie (1948), 20
von Ziegesar, Cecily	Yodelay Uh-Oh (1982), 108
Wesolowska, Monica	No Gushing for Me, Please (1979), 82
Wexler, Laura	The Simple Vase: Part I (1997), 71
Wexler, Rebecca	The Simple Vase: Part II (1997), 74
Whitton, Margaret	On Horseback (1960s), 163
Wiseman, Laura Madeline	A Puddle (1991), 118
Wittenberg, Henrietta	Can I Sit on His Lap? (1916), 96
Yulia	Mattress Pad (1990), 80
Zieman, Kate	I Know You Are Not There, God. It's Me, Kate (1990), 66

Reading Group Guide

1) Which story speaks the most to you? Why? What story most closely resembles your own first period experience? What story is furthest from your own experience?

2) Why do you think that the taboo surrounding menstruation has endured when so many others have already disappeared? In which stories is it most present? What can be done to end this taboo?

3) Contributor Michele Jaffe ("Going to X-tremes") writes that how a girl deals with her first period says a lot about her character and about the woman she will become. Pick a story (some good ones for this exercise are "My Second First Period," "Andy Roddick's Serve," "I Know You Are Not There, God. It's Me, Kate," and "Operation Menstruation!") and discuss how the contributor's reaction to her first period sheds light on who she is. Do you think that is true for your own experience?

4) The oldest contribution for *My Little Red Book* is from 1916 and the newest is from 2007. How have times changed in terms of attitude toward menstruation?

5) Using Gloria Steinem's essay "If Men Could Menstruate" as a springboard for discussion, pick a story and imagine how it would have happened differently had the contributor been a man.

6) Why do we have so many euphemisms for menstruation? What is your favorite?

7) Discuss how the theme of gain being coupled with loss appears in these stories and its relevance to other milestone events in life.

8) Joyce Maynard begins her story "Out of The Closet" by discussing how she was criticized for being "shameless." Why do you think people use this word as a critique? Is being shameless such a bad thing? At the same time, are there still subjects that are meant to be left untouched and unspoken?

9) Some of the contributors express the sense that their mothers just don't get it. Will that ever change? On the flip side, in stories by mothers—for example, "Fear of Fourteen" and "Simple as Salt"—mothers work hard to make sure their daughters' first-period experiences are

better than their own. How do you wish your mother had reacted? If you have a daughter, how did (will) you prepare her for her first period? How do you plan to mark the occasion?

10) If you could have a do-over for your first period, what would you have liked to be different?

11) Several of the stories, most notably "Simple as Salt" and "I Know You Are Not There, God. It's Me, Kate," challenge the common idea that menarche is the transition point from girlhood to womanhood. Do you agree? What were the milestones in your own life that you feel transitioned you from childhood to adulthood?

12) Compare how women experience periods in different cultures.

13) How do girls' relationships with their dads change after menarche? Jenni Deslandes's "Down Under" provides one example. Did your relationship with your dad change?

14) What would be the most embarrassing way you could imagine to get your first period?

15) What perspectives do you think are missing from the collection?

16) Imagine you are your favorite female character in literature or history, and write about a first period from her perspective. A few fun ones might be Joan of Arc, Georgia Nicholson (from *Full Frontal Snogging*), Harriet Tubman, Hermione Granger, Hillary Clinton, and Jane Austen. You are encouraged to submit the story to the www.mylittleredbook.net Web site.

17) Looking at today's sanitary supply ads, is the media solving or perpetuating a taboo? Consider one recent campaign: "Mother Nature calls it your 'monthly gift,' but your period is more like a curse when you need to wear backup, too." At the other end of the spectrum is the "Period Dance" video, which is on Youtube at www.youtube.com/watch?v=r-4APMv2QKo. Do companies have a responsibility to target their ads a certain way?

18) Some birth control pills have made menstruation an optional part of womanhood. Will this lead us to look at womanhood in a different way? Should we keep our periods? Why?

About the Editor

RACHEL KAUDER NALEBUFF was initially embarrassed by her first period, but the power of these recollections has rubbed off. She has come to embrace her own story (and has even used it as a conversation starter). Because she talked about periods . . . let's just say more than once a month, it was inevitable that she would go down in her high school's history as "the period girl." She is absolutely cool with that.

Rachel is currently on a gap year before heading to Yale. In her free time, she plays guitar, rides/falls off her unicycle, and indulges in late-night pie baking with friends. She is donating all the proceeds from *My Little Red Book* to women's health charities so that this book may benefit girls beyond its readers. *My Little Red Book* is her first published work.

To learn more or to contribute your own story, check out www.mylittleredbook.net.

About Twelve
MISSION STATEMENT

TWELVE

TWELVE was established in August 2005 with the objective of publishing no more than one book per month. We strive to publish the singular book, by authors who have a unique perspective and compelling authority. Works that explain our culture; that illuminate, inspire, provoke, and entertain. We seek to establish communities of conversation surrounding our books. Talented authors deserve attention not only from publishers, but from readers as well. To sell the book is only the beginning of our mission. To build avid audiences of readers who are enriched by these works—that is our ultimate purpose.

For more information about forthcoming
TWELVE books,
you can visit us at www.twelvebooks.com.